I0141330

Slightly Skewed

A lopsided look at life,
marriage and family

by

David J. Coehrs

Published by White Feather Press. (www.whitefeatherpress.com)

ISBN 978-1-61808-075-2

Printed in the United States of America

Cover design created by Ron Bell of AdVision Design Group (www.advisiondesigngroup.com)

White Feather Press

Reaffirming Faith in God, Family, and Country!

To Patti, my brown-eyed girl, whose love, devotion, and laughter are the air I breathe.

Acknowledgements

I would like to thank my publisher, Skip Coryell, for offering me the opportunity I always wished for; my sons, Steven and Alex Flack and Justin Reed, who inspire me daily; my late father, Jim Coehrs, and my nine brothers and sisters, who have shared my memories and sparked my imagination; Karen Katafiasz, who long ago made this "different drummer" believe I could; and my mother, Marilyn Coehrs, a writer and poet in her own right, who never, ever doubted that I would.

Contents

Fractions, Dougie and Pink Tights

Sister Mary Gorgonzola was tapping one of her high top sensible nun shoes. "Well, Mr. Coehrs?" she said in that granite nun voice as I fidgeted at the blackboard.

The chalk I held was poised in front of a fraction problem I had no idea how to solve. I wrote a faint 1 in the answer column, and Doug Fitzpatrick laughed.

He was the reigning class math, history, science and spelling king, and because of that got away with murder. If he passed a note, Gorgonzola – or Old Cheesy, as I dubbed her three days into the school year – would pretend not to see. If that wasn't enough, half the girls had crushes on him, and he charged kids a quarter each to watch him blow smoke rings behind the gymnasium from Pall Malls he swiped from his father.

"Mr. Fitzpatrick," Old Cheesy said wearily, "would you please go up and show Mr. Coehrs how to find the correct answer. Otherwise, I fear we'll be here all day."

I wanted to confront her right there, tell her that her black nun's habit with the big white bib made her look like a penguin at the dinner table. But she had one of those heavy wooden clickers that nuns back then used to keep order, and getting whacked across the knuckles with that baby would have taken my arm off at the elbow, leaving me to sell pencils in the streets.

Dougie – which is what the girls called him as he giggled and blushed when he showed off his muscles or a new pair of argyle socks – grabbed the chalk from me and, with exaggerated flair, fired off the correct answer in a nanosecond. Old Cheesy gave a little sound of approval and complimented Doug on both his answer and his socks.

Then she said, "You may take your seat, Mr. Coehrs" in a tone that suggested I had both leprosy and chronic dandruff, which, all right, the second one I did.

Defeated, I sat down at my circa-1930s desk, complete with a hole for an inkwell, and listened to smart-alecky Tom Couzinski next to me mimic Old Cheesy: "Take a seat, Mr. Coehrs!" Being the class clown, he was actually pretty good at it, capturing just the right amount of the Cheese's nasal inflection and squinching up his face like his colon was backed up.

How can a fifth-grader not laugh at that, and so I did, and then ducked down in terror. Old Cheesy had radar like a bat, and I heard her rosary beads clack as she whirled around with a pointed finger.

"Misss-ter Coehrs!" she called loudly in that terrifying way she had, and I slowly poked my head out from under the inkwell hole.

She was absolutely glaring at me, fire shooting out from behind her little round spectacles, which were rimless and had that old-people's dark line running across the middle of each lens.

(Note: The last time I wrote about nuns I got into dutch with my mother, a devout Catholic who was also taught by the good sisters, and who lectured me about the evils of perpetuating those shameful old stereotypes. "Say something nice about them!" she warned.

Naturally, she's right. They weren't all stereotypical nuns. Just those like Old Cheesy. As for saying something nice ... well, the Cheese did have the making of an impressive mustache.)

"Would you care to share with the rest of the class what is so funny?" she said. Every pair of eyes in the classroom turned in my direction, many of them registering shock.

See, I was known far and wide as a goody two-shoes; I was a Coehrs, one of the sickeningly obedient kids who carried reputations for never talking or chewing gum in class or causing disruptions. I was attentive and raised my hand, and I never plugged the toilets in the restroom with entire rolls of paper like "Bad To The Bone Brad" Mueller, who got suspended for drawing pink tights on the statue of our school's beloved patron saint.

"No, I wouldn't like to share, Sister," I said with a blazing face, because how do you tell a nun older than dirt who's taught little brats for 40 years that her face looks squinched, like from colon blockage? Tom Couzinski started whispering "Misss-ter Coehrs!" in a squeaky voice and I kicked him under his desk.

"Well, Mr. Coehrs, then maybe you should stay after school for an hour and think about it," she said, and the whole class gasped. "Bad To The Bone Brad" got after-school detention, but never a Coehrs. It was like a sign of the Apocalypse.

Now I was sweating, because now my dad would find

out. And if my dad found out I would never live to see the Apocalypse.

"Well, Mr. Coehrs?" the Cheese sneered with moldy nun teeth.

"Tom Couzinski imitated you and made me laugh!" I blurted out, and the class gasped again.

Okay, so I traded martyrdom for rat finkdom. At least I didn't give St. Thomas pink tights.

Jonesing for the Sweet Life

IF OUR BANK ACCOUNT WAS A GAS TANK THE FUEL light would always be on. But that didn't stop the woman who controls our checkbook from checking the fares of cruise ships.

Let's back up a bit. This one time in the '80s, when I was still somewhat buff and women didn't recoil in horror, I went with a lady friend on her family's boat to watch Fourth of July fireworks burst majestically over a river. We're not talking about a yacht with half a mile of deck space, either. This was a small, modest cabin cruiser that suited me fine after I dosed up on a couple of her stepfather's signature cocktails, which contained a liqueur so tasty I wanted to lobby Congress to add it to the food pyramid.

We puttered out to the middle of this particular river along with dozens of other boats, and her brother dropped anchor, and we began to roll with the current. Because I had been on the water only once before (a Cub Scout outing – I turned green and ralfed in the pop cooler), and because I had since developed an inner-ear imbalance, I probably should have stayed home and watched the neighborhood kids shoot off bottle rockets.

"Feeling a little skittish?" the stepfather asked, as I clung to my seat and watched the horizon bob up and down, and felt the cocktails swish back and forth in my stomach. To put it mildly, that was not a banner Fourth of July for me. Afterward I stayed away from docks and that liqueur. (Just looking at the bottle now gives me the heaves.)

So when I saw my beloved scanning the computer world for cruise ship rates the memory flooded back and I grabbed a chair to steady myself.

She noticed me, and gave an apologetic smile. "I'm just looking," she assured me.

If I've learned nothing else from our marriage, I know what "I'm just looking" really means. It's part of my wife's extensive codespeak, in which harmless comments actually mean so much more than you wish they did. When she says, "I'm not mad anymore," and I look it up in the code book she gave me on our wedding night, she's really telling me to tread lightly, because she's not above filleting me with kitchen utensils. And when she asks, "What do you think?" it's a signal to agree that she knows best, and not complicate her life with colorful emotions she would otherwise feel obligated to express.

"I'm just looking" needs no translation. It means she has suddenly developed a jones for whatever she's just looking at, and to believe the impulse will pass is like believing Osama bin Laden secretly buys American.

As I watched her taking virtual tours of cruise ships even larger than my prostate, I envisioned the fuel light on our bank account growing steadily brighter.

How she thinks we can afford this is beyond me. After all, she's the one who clips coupons, and warns me under penalty of death not to touch our remaining ten dollars because she has to use it as leverage to finagle a payment extension with the electric company. Their rates have risen so considerably I'm tempted to buy a kite and a big key and go into business for myself.

She motioned me over. "Look. This price is all-inclusive. And there are three ports of call along the way." Besides, I'd have to take motion sickness medicine, and don't like the effects. I've used it for air travel, and I know for a fact those people didn't appreciate me getting all buzzy and singing *Born to be Wild* in falsetto.

"We could do this," my wife said to herself. "This could work." Then, because she heard the groan in my throat, she added, "But really, I'm just looking."

Another time, she was just looking at a late-model camper with a flat-screen TV, Surround-sound stereo, satellite tracking and a pull-out sun deck with pop-up cup holders. We were at one of those auto shows where slinky models drape across car hoods and make white-walls sound erotic. (Not that I noticed.) I could see her beginning to jones, and when she sat on the camper's ergonomically-designed, temperature-controlled driver's seat and actually purred, well, I sort of intuited the looking part was over. We wouldn't have caused a scene if she hadn't kicked and screamed when I carried her out.

I started to edge away from the computer when I heard that purring, low and intense. The virtual tour had reached the 24-hour buffet with pigs on spits, then moved onto the gigantic hot tub with martini bar and towel boy.

"No!" I sputtered. "I'm saying – NO!"

She spun around, glaring. "I'm – just – LOOKING!"

Darn. There go all of my vacation and personal days.

Hey, Dude! Come and Read This!

The 12-year-old keeps calling me "Dude." When I walk in the door it's, "Hey, Dude." When I tell him something he doesn't like, it's, "DUDE!" When I give him good news, he's like, "DOO-HOO-HOOOD!"

I want to know when this whole "dude" thing started. When he was three he called me "Davin" because the D at the beginning was easy but he couldn't quite nail the one at the end. He also said "hangaburg" instead of "hamburger," and "French tries" instead of... well, you get it. And he called anything with spikes or thorns "poiky."

Naturally, we thought it was adorable, and deliberately steered conversations toward those words so he would say them and give us a smile. Once, when I admonished him for bad behavior, he looked at me with teary eyes and said, "Davin, you brolk my feelings." It was so cute I couldn't bear to punish him, and in fact, I recall buying him a car.

Now I enter a room and he's all, "What's happenin' Dude?" and "Whass UP, dude?" Sometimes he accompanies his greeting with a good-natured shoulder punch or a body check, then struts away like the world's his oyster.

These moments always give me pause to reflect on my own father. When I was younger he was pretty much all business. He presided over the house with an air of authority you didn't question, or if you did, well, nobody lives forever. He was old-school, and when he sensed you were going to run roughshod over the rules he would smoke you with a look so venomous my mother kept antidote in the kitchen first-aid drawer.

You can imagine his reaction had I been all like, "Dude! High five!" then popped him one. He wore conservative work pants and shirts, and short, Bryl-Creemed hair, and a favorite family story goes that, because he always bought exactly the same style shoe, we kids thought he'd owned only one pair during our entire childhood. He wasn't the best candidate for "dude."

So you can believe that I also never bopped up to him saying, "Hoo, Big Dog!" or "What's shaking, Daddykins!" or anything even remotely that hip. I would simply call him Dad, and he would respond by asking which one of his ten children I was – he knew it started with a D or T or P.

I never get this "Dude!" stuff from our teenager. He's in his brooding period, which means all you get from him is an occasional grunt and sneering sneers that could vaporize titanium. My wife and I are thinking about hiring him out as the "Before" picture in ads about irregularity.

"Dude!" the 12-year-old yelled when I came home from work. I'd had an excruciating day, what with all the junk food I'd eaten and no time to nap it off. My boss kept me awake with some drivel about my supposed attitude and where it would lead me (the unemployment line) and how I'd better start toeing the line (and he means immediately) or changes will have to be made, and blah blah. At one point, I think I actually fell asleep with my eyes open as he droned on about how I'm expendable, and how he could easily find an iguana who could do my job better. I remember dreaming that I gave him the number of a friend who has a pet iguana and told him to ask for Larry the Lizard. At least, I think I was dreaming.

If I was a younger dad I might not mind "Dude!" as much. I'd be a lot more fun, and wear my hair over my ears, and drive a muscle car, and give my wife hickeys. When I'd hear, "Dude!" I'd answer, "My man!" and do that fist bump thing, then we'd all go out and TP the neighbor's house for laughs.

But I came into fatherhood as an older, more grumpy fellow with one of those boards You-know-where who likes his peace and quiet and a nice rump roast and peas for dinner.

Anyway, the 12-year-old yelled "Dude!" and I'd already had my fill of it for the week.

"I'm not your dude," I replied testily. "I am your stepfather, the pants in this family, your benevolent leader, and I'd appreciate if you'd stop calling me that."

He looked puzzled. "Dude, stop calling you what?"

"Stop calling me "dude."

"DUDE!" he said, offended. "You broke my feelings!"

"Forget it, you're not getting another car," I said. "And using my given name is a matter of respect."

"Dude, don't go all 'Imperial storm trooper' on me. I'll quit calling you 'dude,'" he said.

And he did. Now he has this spiteful twinkle in his eye as he greets me every day with a punch and "Hey, Davin! Want a hangaburg and French tries?"

Dude, it's really getting old.

It Was This or Dancing Penguins

EVERY WORKDAY AT ABOUT TEN IN THE MORNing I stroll an endless, pristine beach. The tide crawls up the sand from the ocean to my left, and shade from an overhanging palm tree offers respite from the blazing tropical sun.

I'm there for a few minutes, basking in the serenity, then I sigh and reluctantly punch the return button on my computer keyboard.

My desk, office and stacks of paperwork swim back into focus, and there's my boss, asking if he pays me for zoning out, and wondering how much I've accomplished since coming in fifteen minutes late and spending what he considered ("... and, believe you me, so would Corporate if I filed a report...") an inordinate amount of time at the break room microwave station.

He claims I fiddled too long there with toasting a bagel, spreading cream cheese on it and mesmerizing Doris from Janitorial with an overly-dramatized discussion of my chronic toe jam condition.

In my defense, the company microwave was probably manufactured around the time Ronald Reagan took office and started falling asleep at Cabinet meetings. You have to mess with the dial to keep your bagel from smoldering after only twice around the carousel dish inside, and that means a complex series of twists like you're opening a combination lock – left to Light, a double spin to Dark, then back until the dial arrow is directly under the U on Medium. Then the cream cheese wasn't the soft, spreadable kind but the hard brick kind that will snap half a dozen cheap plastic knives before you've finished. And Doris has always been fascinated with toe jam. Don't ask me why. She was like that when I started here.

As for the tropical setting I escape to, that's my computer screen saver. It's really beautiful, what with the brilliant white sand and the deep-blue sky and the palm fronds. I selected it over other screen saver choices, like penguins wearing straw hats and doing a funny dance, which, frankly, creeped me out, and a star constellation I should recognize from a college Astronomy class that I skipped every chance I got so I could watch *Three's Company* reruns in the student union.

Which is also why I didn't graduate magna cum laude and score a cake job, with my own parking space and enough money to buy those silk dress shirts with sea horses embroidered on the pockets.

Yes, it's only a screen saver, but the photograph is so enticing to someone like me, who only once in his life was on a tropical beach. That was a lifetime ago, when I bill-collected for a living and earned scads of commission by calling people at ungodly hours and telling them to pay their bills or I'd put hexes on their mothers.

The money rolled in, and I thought nothing of twenty-dollar lunches and designer tennis shoes and vacations to exotic places. That included a Mexican resort with my cousin, seeing how neither of us was setting any fires with girls at home, so we decided to buy revealing swim trunks and head out to dazzle foreign babes.

We were both pasty, and I had a weird multiple wart thing going, and we both weighed about 130 pounds soaking wet, so there wasn't a lot to dazzle anybody with, let alone voluptuous, bikini-clad women with deep tans. So we spent a lot of time in the hotel lounge saying "Dos cervezas, por favor" until our speech got too slurred, and then we would just wave our empty bottles.

So along about ten each day I let the screen saver come on, and I look wistfully at the panoramic view, and harken back to my week in Mexico, which wasn't all bad once I discovered a swim-up bar in the pool.

I remember the turquoise ocean, and the 300-level sunblock I used to avoid frying, and the tour of Mayan ruins, which meant a three-hour drive in a rickety bus through jungle that had bugs the size of your head.

It was a heady week of ogling anything female, and visiting night spots that blared disco music, and spending one unfortunate day indisposed after drinking the local water despite being warned.

I have to view the screen saver discreetly, though, because Doris is not only obsessed with toe jam but also with telling on people.

And I don't need any more black marks on my record. It's just a way to set aside the stresses for a few moments and place myself somewhere soothing and gorgeous, which is certainly not an apt description of where I am, what with assignments piling up and strict deadlines hopping around my work area, and always coming in late because I hit the snooze button each morning until the alarm finally yells back at me to get the heck up.

And because it's almost ten now (actually 9:10, but let's not quibble) I'm going to leave you and dig my toes in the sand and feel that warm breeze on my skin, and do a little daydreaming.

As for my boss, I miraculously managed to get here on time today, and I skipped the bagel and the toe jam, so he can just kiss a duck.

My Kingdom for a Penny!

GREEN GUMBALLS WITH STRIPES WERE ALMOST my ruination

There I was, seven years old, standing in front of the gumball machine at Alma's Market. Alma's was an old-fashioned corner store in my neighborhood. Alma had the gumball machine just inside the front door. Put in your penny, turn the handle and you were rewarded with a round colored ball of pure sugar ecstasy guaranteed to keep a child nice and spastic.

The problem was the special light green gumballs, each with a dark green stripe around the middle. Several were always interspersed among the regular gumballs filling the machine's glass bubble. Getting one was the equivalent of hitting the jackpot. You could turn it over to Alma for one of the small prizes she kept in a cardboard box behind the counter.

Sure, it wasn't the same as winning millions in a lottery or an all-expense paid trip to an island resort where being fairly naked is actually part of the itinerary. That is, not unless you were seven, and getting one of those striped green gumballs was simply one of the most important goals in your limited seven-year-old life.

And it became even more crucial because it seemed like everyone else had already scored a striped green gumball. For criminy sake, my cousin Steve from down the street had scored four of them at once using a single penny because the machine malfunctioned.

Every time I went to Alma's store – about fifty times a day, or until she'd had enough of me – I would stand on tippy-toes and snatch a glimpse of that cardboard box behind the counter, and notice with horror that a lot of the most desirable prizes had been claimed. Then I'd check the gumball machine, tracking the progress of the remaining striped green gumballs as they descended ever closer toward the bottom with every penny.

My need to score a green gumball reached a fever pitch, and like a crack addict looking for a fix I rooted through couches, drawers, my mother's change purse, the floor of our car –anywhere to find even one penny. I lugged in every two-cent returnable pop bottle I could find within a ten-block radius, and even mugged Old Man Steinecke down the street for his penny loafers.

Then Alma would watch with her jaw unhinged as I stood before the gumball machine, sweaty and shaking, dropping my ill-gotten pennies into the slot one by one, turning the handle, hearing a gumball drop into the slot and lifting the lid, my pupils dilated, my heart racing. Red, yellow, blue, orange, yellow, purple, white...

"C'MON, you stupid gumballs," I'd babble. "Gimme a

green one!"

...blue, blue, orange...

"AUUGGGHHHH!"

Then Darryl Binkhauser from around the corner, whose breath always smelled like Nestle's Quik, walked in, bought three cents' worth of licorice whips with a nickel, and used one of the pennies in change to get a gumball.

"AUUGGGHHHH!"

Alma held out the cardboard box, and Darryl selected the one prize in it I'd had my eye on for weeks. It was a little plastic game printed with the heads of *The Beatles* where you'd roll tiny BBs into holes in their eyes.

I ran home and frantically scoured the house for a penny, even one covered with lint or sticky with heaven knows what, but I had cleaned the place out. So, in my desperation, I did what my mother and the old, gnarly pastor at my church would have considered worthy of an express trip to Purgatory.

I quietly entered the corner store, my beady eyes shifting left and right to locate Alma who was busy in the back. I removed from my pocket the round St. Christopher medal I had taken from my brother's dresser drawer – I was seven and thought it would work, sue me – and tried to fit it into the gumball slot. It was just that much too big, but I thought if I pushed a little harder...

It took Alma a week to get the medal dislodged. I got away clean, so no one ever knew I was the culprit. Except maybe Alma, who from then on felt the need to announce "Pennies only!" whenever I showed up.

I never did get a green striped gumball. Darryl Binkhauser let me play with the game he won, but then one of the BBs got wedged in Ringo's eye and Darryl blamed me for it and made me go home. But not before I swiped a penny off his bedroom dresser.

Hollywood People are Plain Weird

If they're not naming their children Apple or Blue Ivy or Pilot Inspektor, or buying third-world babies to raise, they're getting their mugshot taken after a wild night of cavorting and debauchery. If they're not writing juicy, tell-all books that skewer just about everybody they know, they're ending up in the hospital for exhaustion because their lives are so strenuous and difficult. They get paid more for one job than the rest of us do for months of work, or in many cases, an entire lifetime. They're coddled and fussed over but still manage to complain, and they whine over all the attention they get. (Though without it they're lost.)

All the players in that town seem at least a bit off, as though they got dropped once or ten times on their heads. They always seem to have odd ideas about how life and morality work, and about how they're more entitled to everything than the rest of us mere mortals. They act spoiled and petulant, then bemoan the fact they're viewed as spoiled and petulant. And when they're caught doing something particularly heinous they either hide in their multi-million dollar mansions until the dust settles or get probation instead of a well-deserved jail term.

I mention all of this because I want you to know that when I finally find fame and fortune I'm not going to act like that. When someone begins throwing enormous amounts of cash in my direction – so much that I can easily chew up a fresh stack of hundreds in the garbage disposal and not even say "boo" – I'll be the same David I am today, but with custom-made kangaroo leather boots, a Porsche and maybe better smelling breath. I won't go "Hollywood" on you, even after I move there into a 21-bathroom house with its own power plant and zip code. I'll be just plain ol' David, and if you visit me it will be my privilege to have a photo taken with you under my crystal chandelier. And if my overzealous staff sics the attack dogs on you and my bodyguards rough you up, the least I can do is make them pay you fifty bucks for the privilege.

No need to thank me, I'm just that type of guy. I would never allow wealth or fame to change me, unless it's a lot of wealth and fame, and then I might get a little conceited, but really, not much. It would only be enough that I would make the most minor demands on family and friends, such as calling me "Sir" and keeping their heads bowed when they address me, and when I say, "Do these pants make me look fat?" they would reply, "Never, sir. You're built like a Greek god."

It's a matter of remembering where you came from, and what values you hold. I came from a very modest background, one of ten children from the lower middle class, so naturally I connect deeply with the common man and his daily struggles. And when I'm rich and famous I'll always keep my humble beginnings deep within my heart, where they'll remain a constant reminder but won't get in the way if I get caught dating somebody's wife or get into a drunken fistfight in front of paparazzi.

So when I'm rich and famous, by all means, stop by. My door will always be open, and I'll treat you with all the care, affection and down-to-earth geniality you would expect from me. Remember, I'll still be no better than you.

(But if your car is less than, say, a Lexus, park it around the corner so my neighbors won't notice.)

A Fly in the Mouth

10:45 p.m.

I'VE READ THE SAME PARAGRAPH IN THIS BOOK five times, except I haven't really read it because my mind is fuzzy with fatigue. So I follow my brown-eyed girl to bed; she was wise enough to hit the hay earlier when her sleepy head kept falling into her late-night bowl of cereal.

11:30 p.m.

For some inexplicable reason, I am now wide awake, tossing and turning. I know it doesn't make sense, but when have I ever? I was thoroughly wiped out as I brushed my teeth, then slumped exhausted onto my right-side spot, but now my eyes are wide open and I'm actually feeling restless. My brown-eyed girl is snoring next to me, oblivious. I don't think this woman has ever had a problem sleeping. I've seen her crash practically in the middle of dinner, a piece of pork chop hovering on a fork at her mouth as her eyelids droop. All she has to do is eat a filling meal, stretch out to read or listen to me talking, and poof, she's out.

12:10 a.m.

"You gotta be kidding," I mutter as I lie on my back, an uncomfortable position for me to sleep, but I've tried all the others a dozen times. I'm annoyed that she's snoring so loudly, but more so because she's in dreamland and I'm not. I'm tempted to wake her with a nudge, or by dropping a fly in her open mouth, but that would be childish, and besides, I already did that last night. (A nudge. The fly was super big, and creeped me out too much.)

1:57 a.m.

I take a sleep aid, but if anything it makes me wider awake. So I call an old friend to catch up. Apparently, he was asleep too, because he thinks I'm totally wacked for waking him. I hear a lot of groggy shouting, including something about me being out of my mind, which, truthfully, a lot of people have commented on as well during the day. Then he gets downright insulting – something about the horse I rode in on – and yells, "I never liked you that much, anyway!" before slamming down the phone. I don't think I'll call anyone else.

2:41 a.m.

I'm in the kitchen, eating a corn dog slathered with mustard. It's a follow-up to the peanut butter and sauerkraut sandwich, 57 Oreos, 14 cheese sticks, handful of smoke almonds, piece of aging bologna and half a bag of stale beef jerky I've scarfed down over the past forty minutes. As I browse the refrigerator shelves I come across a container with something in it probably no longer identifiable as food. I think, *with lots of ketchup it's worth a try.*

3:22 a.m.

The late-night infomercial hosted by the lead actress of a cheesy '80s drama seems to drone on forever. I'm watching it because I had a crush on her back then, but I don't remember her being this incredibly flaky. Or having had all that plastic surgery and a smoker's cough. Or being platinum blond and trying to hide a poochy stomach under a tight dress. Or wanting to sell me a vacuum cleaner powerful enough to suck up children and unwanted guests.

4:00 a.m.

Back in bed. I have to get up for work in a couple hours. My wife is sawing wood like she's plowing through the entire Black Forest, and one of the cats has decided to lay itself across my prone body. Its eyes are reflective and menacing in the dark, and it's staring directly into mine, as if warning me if I fall asleep it will pounce and eat my liver. I have never trusted cats, so the point is well taken.

6:30 a.m.

The shrill alarm goes off, waking me. I finally fell asleep six and a half minutes ago. My wife bounces out of bed refreshed, and doesn't take kindly to my surly behavior.

"You're such a beast in the morning," she complains. "Why can't you try to be happy, like me?"

Boy howdy. She's getting a fly in her mouth tonight even if I have to go outside and catch one.

David's the Total Bomb

OKAY, OKAY, STOP HASSLING ME. I HAD CLEAN forgotten that today is "Make Up Your Own Holiday" day. And no, you disbelievers, I'm not making that up. In this great country of ours we'll find any reason for a holiday, even if means making stuff up to get a day off. This month also celebrates National Pig Day, National Bubble Week and National Frozen Food Month, and you can bet your sweet petunias I'll be toasting them all.

But I especially like the idea of making up my own holiday. Just as everyone has their own birthday, I think each of us should also have our own customized holiday once a year. It would be a day where, if you wanted, you could sleep until noon, walk around in your underpants, tell people you don't like they're ugly and pathetic and stink like goat cheese, and show people chewed food in your mouth without repercussions. You don't have to go to work, you're allowed to hang up the phone on boring people, and if you walk up to someone and say, "Wash my car and make me French toast" they have to do it.

It would be a great day, where you're allowed to smite all your enemies, which in my case would include Bobby Orloff.

He was older and bigger, in eighth grade, and everywhere I went there would be Bobby. He always pretended it was a happy coincidence, although we both knew he showed up to torment me. He would say, "Well, well, if it ain't Davy Do-Right," a reference to my goody-two-shoes behavior and correct usage of "isn't" rather than "ain't." He would throw a friendly arm around me and lead me into the nearest alley, where he would give me a painful wedgie, steal the emergency dollar out of my sock and tie my shoelaces together. One time I got brave, and told him I'd had just about enough. He decided "just about enough" meant there was room for more, and stuffed me in a trash can.

That wouldn't happen on *David's The Total Bomb Day* which, yes, I'd be allowed to call my holiday even if you think it's a bit egotistical. On my day I would have ninjas track down ol' Bobby and give him what-for, including an industrial-strength noogie and a kick below the bellybutton. I would control the entire day, meaning nothing healthy to eat, with an emphasis on ice cream and those fatty, cholesterol-laden, stomach-rotting chili cheese corn chips my wife is always taking away from me and replacing with carrot sticks. "Talk to the hand," I would say as she protested me scarfing down literally tons of delicious yet flagrantly unwholesome food that would keep me flatulent for days and give me huge pimples. Then I would wear something entirely inappropriate in public and traipse around my neighborhood just because I could. And when uptight Mrs. Dougle with the barky Pekinese came fussing outside to complain, I'd dance around her singing, "I'm too sexy for my thong" and blow her a big, sloppy kiss.

Yes, that's a little out of control, but I'm a firm believer in taking full advantage. Or I was, until my wife began pestering me to instead use my holiday to benefit people and enrich their lives. Don't be such a hedonist, she derided. Don't be so self-indulgent. Spend the day giving something back to your fellow man.

And after considerable thought I agreed, but only on one condition: I still get to do the thong dance. Nothing says you can't be a humanitarian and still shock an old lady and her dog.

Kids on Caffeine – Rhinos on Ex-Lax

TRUE TO MY PROMISE NOT TO INFLAME MY ULcer, I will not call out the 15-year-old on the fact that he has surreptitiously downed five cans of potently caffeinated pop and is now about to send everyone over the brink with his spastic behavior. We're not talking your normal "I've Had a Caffeine Drink And Feel a Bit Jumpy spastic." We're talking about a kid so tightly wound he can't sit down or stop talking more than five, maybe six seconds, tops, not even after being illegally bound to a chair and gagged. (It didn't last long. His mother found him and undid the restraints.)

He knows better than to sneak caffeinated drinks. He knows he's severely restricted lest he scarfs down a few, then gets loose and disrupts civilization as we know it. Or at least shakes up our neighborhood, where he's been tagged "that obnoxious bouncy boy," a description he also goes by at home.

We'll get calls from Craig next door and Old Lady Moody down the street, saying, "Tell that obnoxious bouncy boy to settle down, he's scaring the bejeebers out of us and our pets." I'll hand that assignment over to my brown-eyed girl, and she'll tell him to settle down, but in a mellifluous voice that suggests it's only a suggestion. He'll swing across the room to promise he will, then let out a Tarzan yell and pounce on one of our unsuspecting cats, who will let out a yell of her own, dive onto the couch and scratch the nearest person. (That would be me.)

In his jittery, caffeine-induced state the boy will think that's hilarious, and continue to torment the cat until I yell, "Enough!" while pulling claws out of my arm. "Go outside and annoy the neighbors for awhile. That's what we pay taxes for."

"Butanhouragoyoutoldmetocomeinsidebecausethe neighborskepttryingtohosemedown," he'll babble just like that, without spaces or a breath, forcing his mother to translate for me.

"Forget what I said, and do what I say," I'll tell him, anxious for peace and quiet. "And stay out there for two or three – no, five or six hours. Really give them their money's worth."

I know that's wrong, but I'm beyond trying to win Citizen of the Year. That ship sailed last summer during the infamous Poo War between me and Scotty Pelvington, whose backyard abuts mine. His skeevy little Jack Russell terrier, Gatsby, trotted over every morning to drop presents on my lawn, so I rented a pot-bellied pig, loaded it up with spicy chili and sent it over in the dead of night to perform its magic. Scotty's restraining order against me has just about expired, and after that if I see Gatsby even sniff in my direction I'll rent a rhinoceros full of Ex-Lax.

So after being ordered outside, the boy will yell, "Yes!" and pump his fist before grabbing his ultra-deluxe, authentically-replicated plastic samurai sword and lunging out the front door. Parents up and down the block will pull their children inside, close their blinds and wedge chairs against their doors. "He's loose again," they'll whisper to each other, and arm themselves with pepper spray in case he wanders too near.

"No more caffeine!" we'll tell him after a group of neighbors finally wraps him tight with bungee cord and leaves him on our front porch with a threatening note attached. "The madness stops now!"

And it will, for a whole day. Then he'll visit a friend's house and tap into their caffeine supply.

"TheyaskedmeifIwantedsomeandIwastryingtobepolite," he'll say defensively after the friend's parents have had enough and bring him back hog-tied.

I don't think even he would understand what he said.

No, I Don't Want to Arm Wrestle

He calls them his "guns," and keeps showing them off. The other night he rolled up both sleeves and paraded them around the house, asking if they weren't incredibly awesome, and then answering for me that, yes, they most certainly were.

He flexed them for me, then challenged me to flex mine back. Truthfully, my arms are so skinny I've never really had anything substantial to flex, so I politely declined. "Hah!" he said, as if to validate his point. "My biceps are bigger than yours. Let's arm wrestle!"

I'd forgotten about that. When he was much younger he was always challenging me to arm wrestling. So I'd make a huge production of it, pretending as though he was actually a threat, then letting him win. "I beat him!" he'd crow to his mother. "I'm strong, strong, STRONG!"

Later, when he actually did start getting stronger, I'd still mostly let him win, but occasionally would turn the tables and bring down his arm less than a microsecond after he yelled, "Go!" He would claim I caught him off-guard and demand a rematch, to which I would oblige and let him beat me.

But now he's tall and husky, and has been lifting weights, so the challenge has taken a more serious tone. "C'mon, let's see what you've got," he taunted. (I have to admit his upper arms have developed impressively.) But I figured I still had a few surprises up my own sleeves.

So we cleared the coffee table, interlocked hands and set our elbows in place. We counted down from three, and he charged like a bull, slamming what felt like six Gs of force with his grip. My hand swayed slightly, but then I poured it on as well. Slowly but consistently I pushed his arm backward, until it was just above the tabletop. *He's probably amazed that the old guy still has some grit*, I told myself.

The problem was, my grit wasn't getting his arm to touch the tabletop. I pushed with all my strength but couldn't manage to lay it down completely. I supposed he was determined not to let what he considers an old man best him. So we were deadlocked in this competition, and though my arm felt as if it were being torn off its hinges I didn't give up.

"Now, what's the sense of this?" my brown-eyed girl asked after entering the room. She saw me hunched over, my head inflated three times its normal size from pressure, my tongue protruding like a gnarly Slim Jim, my arm shaking from the battle. The cats surrounded the table, meowing and laying bets against me.

"He thinks he can beat me," the 14-year-old said while casually eating cookies and playing a video game with his other hand.

"You're going to hurt yourself," my wife warned me as my teeth started rattling. "Let go, before you end up in traction."

"I've got him where I want him," I gasped, which even the cats could see was a big, fat lie. "Just give me a minute to finish him off."

"Okay, I'm bored with this," the boy said, and promptly shoved his hand up and over, pinning my arm back onto the table with an audible crack of my knuckles. "Wanna wrestle now?"

He played me. So no, I don't wanna wrestle now. I wanna put my wrenched arm in a sling, then treat both the pain and my bruised ego with an extra strong Rum Booger, which might just give me the liquid courage to challenge him to a rematch.

My wife, who likes to tell me I'm easier to read than a first grade primer, said, "Don't even think about it."

But I have to if I want to win my money back from the cats.

Feline Fun at the Coehrs House

CONTRARY TO POPULAR BELIEF, EVENINGS AT the Coehrs household are not raucous affairs with an open bar and dirty dancing and craps tables, although we like telling people that to make them envious and wish they were as exciting as us.

Truth be told, we sit around in pajamas, munching on fatty snacks we always promise to hate ourselves for later, my eyes transfixed on some numbingly stupid TV show, my brown-eyed girl smoothing the heels of her feet with an egg-shaped device she ordered from late-night television ("And if you act now, we'll DOUBLE this offer! You'll get TWO, a $4,000 value for just $19.99!").

We're not exactly acting like old-age pensioners, although I definitely see us headed in that direction. In a few years I'll probably wear a T-shirt that says, "Retirement means never having to say you're busy," and she'll be in a floral housecoat, hiking up the thermostat to the Char Broil setting and watching Lawrence Welk repeats.

But while we don't dribble oatmeal yet, we're well past the days when she had big hair and I hit the clubs in silky shirts, and stayed unshaven just enough to believe I appeared alluring and edgy to women. The women, on the other hand, would look at the silk and five o' clock shadow combination and mistake me for a sloppy figure skater.

No, we're still young enough to want a little kick to our evenings, and that's where the catnip comes in. The way we see it, our five cats, who range in size from petite to bucking bronco, do their duty well. They spend their days prowling, eating, pooping, napping in inconvenient spots, ignoring us, watching the world from various windows and occasionally fighting each other. They never hesitate to scratch us and everything else in sight when they're moody, or climb out of reach to precarious heights just to tick us off.

So when they knock off at the end of a hard cat day, I will sometimes break out the catnip – to reward them, sure, but mainly for the fun and inexpensive floor show.

All they have to do is see me reach into a particular kitchen cabinet and they know what's coming. "Catnip! Swee-e-e-e-t!" they'll meow to each other, and start landing high fives and jockeying to get more than the others. This causes some hissing and raised hair as they argue: "Oldest first!" "No, biggest first!" "Nuh-uh, cutest first!"

"Relax," I tell them as they pace anxiously. I'll pinch equal measures out of the bag and they pounce on their shares like ravenous tigers. It takes only a couple of minutes for the cheap thrill to hit them. Five distinct cat personalities that sometimes clash into flying fur and high-pitched yowls are suddenly way cool, man, just chillin' and rolling around with glazed eyes in a love fest cat circle. You can practically read their minds:

Calico cat: "Wow, man! I'd bite everybody if I didn't suddenly love you all so much."

Gray cat: "Right back atcha, honey. Peace out."

Petite cat: (sigh) "I'm floating on air."

Orange cat: "Kisses to all!" (smacker smacker)

Tabby cat: "Does anyone else see three of everything?"

They get so mellow it tempts me to give catnip to our boys, too:

"I love you, dude. Let's not fight, and you can have all my stuff."

"You too, dude. How about a hug?"

Maybe when their mother isn't around.

Zombies and the Creep Factor

A PRAYING MANTIS CAN TURN ITS HEAD LIKE A human, and, gaw, that just creeps the living creep out of me. It's not enough that the female mantis devours her mate, but knowing that afterward she can turn her head like a person, look at me and say, "Needed salt" makes my heebie-jeebies twist and shout. I mean, here's this ugly, spindly green thing (although from its perspective I'm probably no prize either) that can turn its head almost 180 degrees to look for its next meal or to tell the kids in the back seat to shut up while it's driving. It already walks kind of human – granted, like one that has had about 15 cocktails – so being able to turn its head just ups the creep factor. And I don't need anything more to creep me.

For instance, there's this shaving cream commercial that shows a close-up view of individual whiskers on a chin, and they all have human faces. Well, after my praying mantis revelation I sure didn't need to see that. Human faces superimposed on inanimate objects give me the willies, just like clowns give me the willies. I have never seen a clown that didn't raise the hair on my neck, so when about thirty of them come bounding out of one of those little circus cars I have to lie down right there in the stands and have a heebie-jeebie fit until someone covers my eyes.

And while we're on the subject, I'm also freaked by the glass eyes on porcelain dolls. Go ahead and laugh, but next time you see one notice the blank, spooky stare that follows you everywhere. It's the same stare you get from movie zombies right before they munch on somebody's spinal column, and the one I get from the boys every time I ask if they have homework, or have finished cleaning those toxic waste dumps they call bedrooms like I asked them to four hours earlier. That zombie stare terrifies me, whereas the boys' stare just gives me acid reflux.

And sunflowers. They look like huge alien eyes. Enough said. But what really makes my flesh crawl are swarms, whether they be bees, locusts, ants, rats or Shriners. There's something about all those bodies in chaotic motion, frenetically writhing and climbing over one another that makes me gag worse than when watching Newt Gingrich try to act intelligent.

No, I don't know why I'm like this. But I do know that everyone has their quirks. Like the college friend of mine who held pop cans with just the tips of his fingers at the top and bottom because he feared wrapping his hand around one would make the beverage warm. Or a past female co-worker who wore only garish, ankle-length skirts for any and every occasion, even to play softball. Or the guy I knew who liked to stick used chewing gum in the coin returns of vending machines.

So at least I'm not alone. And I think I read somewhere that people with boatloads of quirks usually test out at the genius level, and stand a much better chance at schmoozing with the rich and famous and being named one of *People* magazine's fifty most interesting and sexy people.

I'm pretty sure I read that somewhere. But even if I'm making it up – which I'm not admitting to and you can't prove – it sounds really good, and diverts your attention from another quirk of mine involving bathroom procedures.

And you thought the doll eyes thing was weird.

Wake Me Up Before You Go Go Crazy!

LAH LAH - LA LA LAH LAH - LA LA LAH LAH LAH LAH LAH!

It's in my head, and I can't get it out. I'm breaking into a cold sweat, and I think I'm going to crack.

Lah lah - la la lah lah ...

I heard the commercial jingle three days ago. THREE DAYS AGO! ... la la lah lah LAH LAH LAH! AND IT WON'T LEAVE ME ALONE!

The song was so cloyingly cute and oddly creepy I told my wife I would never buy the stupid thing being advertised, even it someone put a gun to my head. Now I'm wishing someone would do just that.

The lyrics accompanying the melody are just as annoying, like fingernails scratching at my brain. And because it's a children's product the song is sung by kids. Cutesy, happy kids.

I'm thinking of using our electric can opener to slice open my skull so I can dig in and yank out this torture. The only problems with that idea are, 1. My wife is using it right now to open cans of tuna, which means my frontal lobe would smell fishy afterward, and 2. From previous experience, I know when the opener spins my head in a circle I'll get dizzy.

Some songs are demonic this way. They're just catchy enough that they stick in your mind and refuse to let go. So you walk around, not even realizing you're quietly singing it (Lah lah - la la lah lah ...) over and over, until you realize people are treating you like you're psychotic and giving you lots of space. But when you try to stop singing it you realize you can't. It's like an invasion, and the music and lyrics form a loop in your head that plays over and over and over.

So you try to break the cycle by thinking of other things: I want a chocolate malt that won't make me fatter. I want a winning lottery ticket I don't have to tell anyone about. I want to know which cat left a surprise in my shoe.

And this actually works for awhile, bolstering your confidence that you finally licked the devil song, which in turn makes you think of the devil song, and next thing you know, Lah lah - la la lah lah ...

This has happened to me with catchy tunes before: *Wake Me Up Before You Go-Go* (lasted Eight Days.) The *Gilligan's Island* theme (19 days.) The *Chicken Dance* tune, which landed me in solitary confinement until I shut up. You wake up, and there it is, in your head. So you sing it in the shower; and between bites of breakfast; and at work, where you tap out the beat with a pencil; then you hum it at dinner, where everyone grips their steak knives tightly, telling themselves not to do it – it's not worth a prison sentence; then softly in your spouse's ear, which doesn't have nearly the romantic effect you figured; then later, while brushing your teeth, during which time your family secretly confers about sending you far, far away.

And now it's been three days of this latest insanity. Three

days, and my brown-eyed girl has locked herself in our bedroom and threatened to call an exorcist if I don't, for corn's sake, stop singing that creepozoid song. The 14-year-old, who is annoyed by everything, including himself, caught himself singing it under his breath and screamed in terror. The cats keep yowling it, then attacking each other. A pair of policemen came to our door with a cease-and-desist order from our neighbors, and left humming it in two-part harmony.

Heaven help me, I'm infecting everyone.

Happy Marriage? Focus on the Wart

"MOM, DO YOU THINK IT'S WRONG TO TELL your kids, 'I told you so?'"

That was one of our boys. I was busy picking up after him for the umpteenth time, and correcting him for it for the umpteenth time. In the midst of my venting I mentioned that I can't wait until he has children of his own so I can gloat, "I told you so!" "Then you'll see," I groused. "Then you'll understand."

That's when he unloaded his question on my brown-eyed girl. And that's when she surprised me with her answer. "Yes," she said, "I think it's wrong to tell your kids, 'I told you so.'"

Before I knew it, I was yelling, "HAH!" loud enough to startle the cats out of their naps.

"Something on your mind, dear?" my wife asked, knowing full well that merely asking that question can send me on a three-hour diatribe. Usually, before she asks if something is on my mind, she'll first set up her zoning out technique, which comes in super handy when I go off on a tangent.

Here's how she does it. When I begin spouting off about my latest grievance (Who ate all the chocolate chip cookies? Why can't I ever get in the bathroom? How the heck are we supposed to pay for that?) she'll concentrate all her attention on a tiny wart I have on my forehead. Within thirty seconds the tiny wart has her as mesmerized as a tiny wart can, which, frankly, is enough when your choice is either that or listening to me drone on in perpetuity. She'll fix that blank forehead stare on me as I go jabbering on and on about this subject or that, and when my lips finally stop moving her brain releases her from the tiny wart and she'll say, "Yes, I can see your point," and we're done until my next blab session.

One time, I noticed the tiny wart in the mirror, and mentioned that it seemed unsightly, and maybe I should have it removed, That's when my wife yelled "NO!" loud enough to startle the cats out of their naps. She tried to explain to me how vital the wart is to keeping her sanity around me, a concept I was too dense to understand but still kind of took offense at. She settled the issue by saying when I'm on a rampage she has to have either the tiny wart or heavy tranquilizers, and she doesn't need a prescription for the wart.

But as I was saying, I responded "HAH!" when my wife rejected "I told you so." I told our boy that's the sole reason I have waited anxiously for him and his brothers to experience marriage and children. Not only to cut our food, water and electric bills by half, but so I can pursue my God-given right to watch their own kids drive them crazy, then say, "I told you so."

"It's what keeps me going," I told him. "Each time you leave a dirty dish to grow moldy under your bed; each time I have to step over your shoes; each time you drag stuff out of your room and leave it stacked on the living room couch; each time your clothes end up hanging off a lampshade; each time I tell you something fifteen times and you still don't listen, I think of you surrounded by kids who inherited those genes from you, and I gleefully tuck away another "I told you so" for future use. After all this frustration, it's my right. And I CAN'T WAIT."

"Just ignore him and stare at his wart," my wife advised the boy.

And my ranting woke up the cats again. Poor things never get any sleep.

Ferrets, Toilet Tanks and My Brown-eyed Girl

We pull up to another house, looking over the junk piled at the curb. "Nope," my brown-eyed girl says. "Keep moving."

I drive away, begging her to stop this madness. "Are you kidding?" she replies. "Think of the money we'll save."

She makes a false sighting at a house two doors down. It causes her to jump from our moving car and walk over for a closer look.

"Darn!" she says, hopping back in. "I thought we had one."

It's the first of two annual unlimited pickup days, when the garbage men will accept more than the regulated trash. They'll take things like old furniture and appliances and various machinery, and you could probably stick an elephant with an obvious hygiene problem on the curb and they'd take that, too. One day when I'm rich enough to afford such an elephant I'm going to try it.

It's also a wonderful opportunity to learn interesting facts about your neighbors. For instance, who'd have thought that Big Merv, the brawny Harley guy across the street who everyone knows paid too much for his split-level, would drag a seven-foot-tall ceramic beaver wearing a top hat, tails and a cheesy buck-toothed grin to the curb. It's fascinating to think that a disgruntled single man with too much body hair and an arm tat that says "Death to Pansies" was sitting at night, drinking and watching NASCAR on television with that creepy thing keeping him company.

Meanwhile, the scavengers have emerged. They troll slowly through the neighborhood in trucks and vans, looking for hidden treasure among the junk piled at the curbs. I find this highly entertaining, and will usually eat all my meals on our front porch and rent a Port-A-Potty so I don't miss even a minute.

That's what I usually do. This time, however, it's my wife and me doing the trolling. We're looking for toilet tank covers. One of ours broke, and my sweetie can't possibly understand why we'd buy a new one when there must be dozens, heck, even thousands of used ones buried among the flotsam and jetsam on everybody's curbs. All we have to do, she figures, is grab two or three different models and lug them home and try to fit one to our coverless toilet tank.

She explains it in a reasonable way, and I do give her props for wanting to save money. But I find two things wrong with her plan: 1. We're driving around looking for someone else's scurvy old toilet part, and 2. We're doing it in our neighborhood, where gossip is like a crack addiction, and in the short time we've lived here I've already given the neighbors enough to talk about. (Believe me, I tried to explain that the awful incident with the garden hoe and the pet ferret next door was purely an accident.)

But that doesn't dissuade my wife, and three houses up we spot the remains of a commode whose crumbled base looks like the victim of someone who packed in too many chocolate malts. The tank cover is intact, though, and my wife brazenly walks into the yard and removes it, carrying it over her head like she just won a heavyweight championship belt. On the other hand, I have scooted down in my seat wearing a low-brimmed hat and huge black sunglasses.

We reach home an hour later, and she stages another show by pulling three different toilet tank covers from the back seat and carrying them to the house while I slink behind her with my shirt pulled over my head. Their clanking in her arms alerts our nosier neighbors, who gather in a cluster to watch, whispering, "Now, what do you think that's all about? You know, the husband attacked a ferret with a hoe."

Once inside, I look through the front window and notice Big Merv sitting on his porch, eating a meal, a Port-A-Potty behind him. You can't blame him for not wanting to miss even a minute.

Superior Parenting Through Duct Tape

REPORT CARDS ARE HANDED OVER, AND THREE boys face us as if we're a firing squad. From their worried expressions it's a sure bet their mother and I will not like what we see. That means another round of grounding them from everything but breathing.

I inhale deeply, and they flinch. They know the Salesman Story is coming, which for them is worse than a firing squad, or for that matter being dissolved by acid-dripping aliens. Even my wife throws me her "I'm begging you, not again" look, but when I'm in the mode to teach a humbling life lesson nothing short of one of those acid-drippers can stop me.

I look down, slowly close my eyes for effect, and use my best hard-boiled voice as I begin: "They were size 6 pumps, and I was a shoe salesman ..."

A member of my audience immediately cracks under the strain of having endured this too many times. "I can't hear you – la la la!" is being yelled over my voice.

It's my wife. Her hands are covering her ears, and she looks wild-eyed and ready to bolt if I say another word. The boys aren't fazed by her behavior because they've been there. So to show them I mean business I calmly duct tape their mother to the floor.

"I stretched those demon size 6 shoes mercilessly on a mop handle in the back room of the shoe store, pulling and tugging until my ribs threatened to burst. The Amazon woman who chose them wore at least a Shaquille O'Neal size, but wouldn't admit it. I was torturing the poor high heels so I could make a sale, just one sale, so I could afford to eat before I settled for the night at the homeless shelter.

"Meanwhile, the woman stood near the rack of fancy shoe polish and designer laces, looking like Mount Everest wearing a polka-dot blouse, smacking lemon-lime gummy candy and impatiently tapping her feet. Which, by the way, were already crammed so tightly into a too-small pair of shoes she groaned like a rhinoceros with pinkeye.

"I was in my twenties, trying to make a living. My boss was a crabby old goat with bad breath and a worse toupee. I hadn't earned a commission since I'd been hired. The retail racket wasn't my thing, and touching customers' crusty feet all day wasn't exactly a picnic with fried chicken.

"I had wanted to be a writer since I was twelve years old, the year I got a B-minus on a poem I composed in Creative Writing class.

I look expectantly at the boys. They sigh, and recite the poem from memory:

"I love a girl in a checkered dress/But she hates me, I must confess/So I will win her hardened heart/When Cupid shoots his magic dart (in her neck)."

"That's when I knew," I continue dramatically, as my wife tries frantically to free herself. "That's when I knew I could be a writer, if only I worked hard and did well in school." I give the boys more steely eyes. "But, no-o-o-o, I was too busy playing around and having fun to take my education, my career and my life seriously. I didn't try, and I got report cards like these.

"And do you know what happened to me, the young boy who could have become a zillionaire writer, if only I had paid attention in school and done better? Ten years later I was living in a shoebox, eating bugs off car windshields and trying to fit a small shoe on that candy-smacking Bigfoot."

I end with a dramatic flourish, and wait for them to sob and grab my legs, begging for another chance. Instead, they look at me like I just ate a cockroach in front of them.

"Do you understand what I'm trying to say?" I ask. "Should I tell the story again?"

"NO-O-O!" their mother screams, finally pulling a foot loose. "I'll do better, I promise!"

One day soon, this lesson will finally sink in. They'll come home from school anxious to show me fists full of A-pluses and gushy letters of congratulations from their teachers. They'll be determined to prove themselves worthy and on the path to success.

Because if they don't, I've been saving my Minimum Wage Telemarketer Story.

But first I'll tape them to the floor.

The Wrath of Mom

WANT TO KNOW WHY I HATE WINTER? "Dude, I'm so-o-o-o bored."

That's our youngest boy. And that's the twentieth time he's made that announcement in the last hour. He's sprawled on the couch like a deflated parade float, idly kicking his brothers, who are this close to reaching level 246 on their video game, and not in the mood to be aggravated.

"Quit it!" one of them says, aiming his own kick. "If I mess this up I'm going to destroy you."

"No destroying," I warn him. "And before you even think about it, no eye-gouging, wedgie-giving, karate-chopping or frying pan-whacking."

I'm trying to read a book, which, without their constant interruptions, I could easily finish by dinner time. But I have kids, which means I'll finish it sometime after I'm dead.

The temperature outside is 467 degrees below zero, and I defy anyone to say I'm exaggerating. My car is frozen and won't start, and that annoying, yippy neighborhood dog I hate is stuck by his icy stream of pee to a tree.

After trying vainly to fire up the old heap I run back into the house and shed the dozen layers of clothing my wife insisted I wear out there so, once back inside, I'd still be thawed enough to do housework.

It's the coldest day so far this winter, with news programs advising everyone to stay instead and inject hot chocolate directly into their veins. So the five of us are trapped together. Although, held hostage is a better description.

We're a tight family, but being stuck in close quarters has its limits. I can predict exactly what's going to happen:

Within half an hour the boys will be clubbing each other with household objects, including the cats. It will start as fun, then morph into a full-fledged battle with lots of red faces, jumping on furniture and crashing into things while they scream liked banshees and ignore my warnings that someone is going to get hurt, darn it, so knock it off. Then that someone I warned them about will start yelling, "OW! I'M TELLING MOM!"

The Grand Household Poobah, Ruler Of All That Was Once Mine And Is Now Supposed To Be Ours But Somehow Has Become Totally Hers, will now enter the scene. Three boys will freeze in place, one with what resembles our curtain rod still held in attack mode. I'll crouch in a dark corner with the book plastered to my face, trying to be invisible. The ruckus will have awakened her from her nap, and all of us know that death is preferable to facing her wrath.

With lightning speed her finger will jab at us, one by one. "Sit, sit, and sit!" she'll howl at the boys, and hiss "C'mere!" at me. The scorching heat of her groggy mood will instantaneously singe the cats, melt candles, and hike the room temperature twenty degrees.

While the boys sit terrified, slapping the hot spots out of their clothes, and shifting their remorseful eyes toward

Heaven, I'll get The Talk. She'll try to deliver it calmly and civilly, but her nostrils will smoke as though she's electing a pope, and I'll know the mother in her wants to smack me silly.

She'll begin with how I can't allow this type of thing because someone could get hurt, and – Whaddaya know? – someone did. She'll say how I need to stay on top of these boys, because otherwise they'll act like savages and grow up to rob convenience stores and poke old men in the eyes. They won't respect our authority, and when we grow old they'll nail us into the attic and feed us moldy oranges and asbestos through the door crack.

Show them alternatives, she'll say. Lead them in quiet, fun, safe projects that won't wake her up. Because we both know that when momma ain't happy...

... ain't nobody happy, I'll finish obediently, patting the sparks out of my hair.

Then she'll go back to lie down, and I'll storm back into the room with my I Dare You To Push Me One More Inch dad face. I'll grab my book and sit down angrily, hard enough to raise a cloud of dust because I haven't been regularly cleaning it with the vacuum attachment, which is supposed to be my job. The boys will fight giggles because I got yelled at, then respectfully wait about five minutes before starting the whole thing over again.

And that's why I hate winter. I much prefer summer, when the boys have more room to beat each other to a pulp in the fresh air and sunshine.

The Power of Barkeeps and Crunchy Bits

THE BARKEEP THINKS I HAVE ABOUT SEVENteen screws loose, which some days isn't so far wrong, but I don't want him spreading it around. He grabs the bowl and tells me vociferously to put them back or else.

Seeing as how I'm a grown man full of rum, he's not going to do much of anything but continue this tirade. He curses both the heavens and my lowly Uncle Bob, which, I don't even have an Uncle Bob, lowly or lofty, but he doesn't seem to care.

Remember that this all started because I picked all the crunchy bits out of the bar mix at my favorite tavern. I like the piquant combination of bar mix ingredients just fine, but the crunchy bits really speak to me because they have a whimsical, garlicky flavor I find especially appealing. So as I waited for the barkeep to blend my next Rum Booger I systematically nudged through the bowl of bar mix in front of me and removed all the crunchy bits.

Believe me, it wasn't the act of defiance he imagined it to be. Every time I've eaten bar mix I've always gone straight for the crunchy bits because they're my favorite. I guess it's a bit selfish of me, but I have a jones for the crunchy bits the way some people do for crack cocaine or the World Wrestling

Federation.

I had them lined up in rows in front of me, like a crunchy bit army, when the barkeep returned with my Rum Booger. He stopped abruptly.

"What do you think you're doing?" he asked, his jaw unhinged.

"I'm eating bar mix," I said, popping two of the little soldiers in my mouth.

"You picked out all the crunchy bits. You can't do that."

"But they're my favorite."

"Look, pal, you have to eat all of the bar mix. That means the beer nuts and the weird round stuff and those hard things that look like tiny pumpernickel bread slices."

"Can I have a bowl full of just the crunchy bits?"

He looked at me like I had just asked him to put on a Speedo and do a pole dance.

"No, you can't have a bowl full of just the crunchy bits," he said, sweeping the crunchy bit rows into his hand and tossing them into the bowl. "You have to eat the beer nuts and the weird round stuff and the hard pumpernickel breads too, just like everyone else."

"What if I pay extra for just a bowl of the crunchy bits?"

Then he looked at me like I was an alien with two heads and six eyes. "Are you trying to cause trouble? Just eat the honkin' bar mix the way God intended."

I'm of the mind that God also prefers the crunchy bits, so I bided my time until the barkeep left to take a drink order. Then I quickly picked them out of the bowl again, wrapped them in a bar napkin and stuffed them out of sight.

Since then he has returned, and eyed the bowl. "Where's all the crunchy bits?" he asks.

"Beats me," I reply sarcastically. "I've been busy enjoying the succulent beers nuts, weird round stuff and hard pumpernickel things."

"Give them back," he says, hands on his hips.

"Why don't you accuse that guy?" I ask, pointing to an old man nursing a beer. "He looks like a crunchy bits thief."

Red-faced, he grabs the bowl and shakes it in my face. "Listen, you loon! Put them back, or else."

The Rum Boogers make me brave. "Or else what?" I challenge him.

"Or else, by God and your lowly Uncle Bob, I'll throw you out of here!"

"Over crunchy bits?"

He grabs me by my shirt. "They're my favorite, too!"

Funny, I figured him for a World Federation Wrestling kind of guy.

Poetic Prankster Justice

I WAS THIRTEEN YEARS OLD, WITH A GROUP OF friends on a Friday night. We're at Patrice's house, and Tom is on the telephone with someone whose name he randomly selected from the white pages.

"Can you come and get me?" he asks in a squeaky voice. "I'm lost, and I'm scared."

The person asks where he's calling from. "It's a small house made of gingerbread in the woods," Tom says. "A mean lady is putting a kid in her oven."

Click.

We laugh, then it's Carol the Braniac's turn. She closes her eyes, drops her finger onto a name in the book and dials the number. When someone answers she adopts a cultured, professional tone.

"Sir, this is the law firm of Botchki, Botchki and Florentine. We are representing a Miss Hester Manfingers, who claims that you urinated on her automobile tire."

She listens for a moment, then gives us a thumbs-up signal. The person bit. "According to the document before me, you are being sued by Miss Manfingers for criminal damage, trespassing and littering. Yes sir, littering. Because you littered your urine."

Margie, whose parents would kill her if they knew what we are doing, gets a fit of giggles. She's a naive goody two shoes like me, and feels both wicked and excited being part of this.

Now Jeff is starting to laugh, and slaps his hands over his mouth. Everyone gives him a warning look.

"Mr. Botchki asked me to contact you to arrange a settlement agreement for his client so this does not proceed to court." The Brainiac perfectly maintains her composure. "Yes, sir. Urination is a Class Two felony. You are a urine felon."

The rest of us don't know what a felon is, but it sounds great, and it makes the man on the phone raise his voice.

"Really, sir, that type of language is odious," Carol says, stifling a chuckle. We look at each other. Odious? Did she make up that word?

The man hangs up, and we laugh about urine for several minutes before the phone is unexpectedly pushed toward me. I'm not good at this. My sheltered upbringing did not include crank calls to perfectly nice people about their urine-soaked activities. This gathering is new territory for me, a peer pressure I've succumbed to because I want to prove I'm not the nerd everyone knows I am. I look to Margie for support, but she's trying to raise her "cool" quotient, too. I'm afraid to call a stranger and abuse them. I just know they'll have a call-tracing device and I'll be hunted down. Police will burst through Patrice's front door with guns drawn, I'll have to go downtown handcuffed and blubbering in front of classmates, and the crank call will go on my permanent record. The nuns at school have repeatedly warned us about tarnishing our permanent records. We won't be able to go to college or get a job or get married, and we'll end up under a bridge somewhere trying to sell stolen goods and eating weeds for dinner.

Everyone looks at me expectantly, and Tom is smirking because he thinks I'll back down. So I nervously grab the telephone and try to act brazen while dialing a number from memory. Someone picks up, and I take a deep breath and start in: "I'm from a lawyer, and you're a urine felon, and I think I'll sue you. Huh? Uh, no this isn't me. No, Grandma, this isn't me. No, I don't think this is even one bit funny ... I called you because I didn't want to call a stranger ... No, Grandma, you don't have to tell them ... Please don't tell them, Grandma!"

Forget the permanent record, now I have to face my parents. On the other hand, my call got the biggest laugh all night.

Big, Fat, Dribbly Lies

DURING A TRIP TO NEW YORK STATE SOME years back my dad was pulled over by a state trooper. He had been cruising through a state park at a speed not exactly considered reasonable anywhere in the world when lights starting flashing behind him.

My mother, who has never, ever broken the law (or at least never admitted to it) immediately flipped out. She yelled at Dad to, for heaven's sake, PULL OVER! From her shudder he could tell she was imagining all sorts of intrusive strip searches and criminal line-ups, and jail time with women covered with tattoos who wouldn't think twice about calling her a hussy and shoving past her in the chow line.

"I told you not to speed," she said with that special tone she reserved just for him. "I've told you for an hour that you're speeding, and to slow down. 'Slow down,' I said, and now we're going to be arrested and strip-searched, and I have old underwear on. I don't know about you, Speed Demon, but I don't want this on my permanent record!"

Dad had received his share of major traffic violations in the past (Sir, I understand the children were driving you crazy, but it's illegal to make them ride on the hood) so this stop was small potatoes. "Don't worry," he told my mother.

"Just let me handle it. I get out of tickets all the time."

My mother was about to say, "What do you mean, all the time?" when the trooper exited his vehicle and sidled up along Dad's window. My parents could practically see a ticket for a bazillion dollars appearing in his hand.

There was a cheesy grin on Dad's face as he handed the guy his driver's license and registration without being told. Then Dad started weaving this incredible tapestry of excuses and half-truths, which poured from his mouth like honey and he accentuated with a sparkle in his eyes. The trooper stood grim-faced as he heard phrases like 'No kidding, that fast?' and 'I didn't even realize!' and then some manure about how the speed gauge must have been stuck on thirty since Pennsylvania.

The trooper started shifting uncomfortably on his feet, as though he was pulling a double and suffering an almost hemorrhoidal case of Raging Road Butt, so Dad went to Plan B. He brought out a photo of we kids taken specifically to get him out of jams, the one where we're dressed in rags in a shanty town, cooking dog on a spit.

"We're all they've got," Dad said weepy-eyed and with a quiver in his voice. He motioned to himself and my mother, who at that point was wondering if maybe a little prison time away from him would be a blessing.

The trooper was obviously ready to clock out and head home to eat spicy nachos and drink about forty-seven beers in front of the tube. There's no other way to explain his acceptance of Dad's clearly big, fat lies and dribble, which, if you traveled to the far ends of the earth, you would still never again hear such big, fat, dribbly lies.

I mention all of this because I am currently pulled over

on the freeway, and a trooper with no visible signs of Raging Road Butt is approaching my window.

The boys had been acting up in the back seat, slugging each other and spilling the snacks my wife and I thought would keep them from going feral. When I leaned back to tell them to knock it off or I would leave the steering wheel and come back there – my foot pressed hard on the gas. That shot us forward so that we almost smacked into the back end of a really expensive sports car with a bumper sticker that said in tiny letters: If you can read this we're probably already trading insurance information.

Well, wouldn't you know the aforementioned trooper just happened to have set up a speed trap nearby, where he saw the whole sordid incident, and lit up his overheads.

"Great," my wife said. "You never get out of tickets."

"Just let me handle it," I say, although I'm already calculating the fine and wondering how much I'll have to kiss up before it sounds like begging. When the trooper reaches my window I'm already holding out my driver's license, registration and proof of insurance, a sickening smile on my face from ear to ear. I compliment him on his shiny boots.

"Double shift, I'll bet," I say cheerfully. "Bet you can't wait to go home and put up your tired dogs and eat you some spicy nachos with about forty-seven beers. Well, who deserves it more?"

His smile is as huge and insincere as mine as he writes a citation that will take me years to pay. The boys think it's funny. They won't, though, as soon as we're out of sight of the trooper and they're all on the hood.

Tim Allen has Nothing to Fear From Me

YESTERDAY A SHELF FELL DOWN IN OUR BEDroom closet. I immediately blamed the mishap on poor craftsmanship, but my brown-eyed girl knew better. She pointed out with plenty of condescension that you can't keep heaping heavy stuff atop something attached to the wall by penny nails and expect it to stay up.

"Well, duh," I said, trying to act like one of those TV handy guys. She had tried several times to warn me. Maybe a cheap plastic shelve isn't the best place to display your bowling ball collection, she said. But I sneered with the kind of testosterone-soaked bravado men like to wave around when they think they're right, which always seems to swing back and bite their heinie right in front of the one person who knew all along they were just being dumb.

The problem is, now she expects me to reattach the shelf. This morning she stood with one hand on her hip and the other holding out a hammer. She was giving me her disgruntled wife look, which, after years of marriage, I have finally learned to tolerate after downing six or seven strong cocktails.

She knows so much better than to expect I can actually do this. My skill as a handyman is equal to my skill as a stripper. Just take my word for it: If you're going to slide around that pole, you should slather yourself with baby powder or it will be a long night.

I'm so ignorant and incompetent as a fix-it guy I'd probably face corporal punishment just for wielding a tool. If I so much as touch one an alarm should go off and I should be poked hard with a ... what do yo call it? ... you know ... one of those things ... it's long and sharp and ... there used to be one in my dad's tool box, for God's sake. I've never figured out what it's called or used for, but a hard poke from one would really hurt.

Apparently, Tim Allen of *Tool Time* has nothing to fear from me.

Beware the Flapping Ball-cock

This is really kind of embarrassing. Our society assumes guys are pulled from the womb wearing a tool belt and knowing how to use a three-eighths-inch drive socket set. People take for granted that when one guy says to another, "If you're going to install ceiling tile always go with furring strips" the meaning will be understood without using a translator.

Besides, my beloved is the handy one. While I was at work one night she assembled a huge do-it-yourself entertainment center, spackled the house from top to bottom and designed an energy-efficient hutch for our pet bunny. When a hinge comes loose or that floaty toilet thingy goes on the fritz, she's your man.

We stand side-by-side in the bathroom, peering into the porcelain tank. "The problem is a worn ball-cock assembly," she announces, shaking her head. "And we'll probably need to replace the flapper valve."

"Yeah, the ball-cock assembly," I repeat, staring at toilet innards. "And the flapper valve. Hmmm."

"I'll have to run to the hardware store," she says. "It would help if you took apart the assembly while I'm gone."

"Yeah, take apart the assembly," I mutter, having no clue

what I'm looking at. I try to sound knowledgeable. "Sounds good, uh-huh. I'll just take apart that assembly and double-check that flapper thing. Can't have it flapping all over the place."

"It's supposed to flap," she says.

"I know," I lie. "I just don't want it to overflap. Wow! Imagine the danger!"

She studies my face. "You have no clue what is going on here, do you?"

"Sure, sure," I say. "A flapping ball-cock valve. I can replace one with my eyes closed."

She sighs heavily. 'On second thought, don't touch anything until I get back. Don't even look at or breathe on anything. And, for corn's sake, stay out of the tool box."

So while she's gone I sit on my hands and try to behave, but she has bruised my fragile male ego. It keeps yelling indignantly in my ear that whatever she can do mechanically I should do better. And it's taunting me to grab what I think is a wrench and show her what's what in Toilet Land.

By the time she returns I have removed everything that looks flappy or even faintly resembles an assembly, plus a few bolts that looked like fun to turn.

"Aren't you proud of me?" I ask, holding the parts as the room fills with water.

I was right. A poke from one of those long, sharp things does really hurt.

The Obligatory Crazy Neighbor

YOU WOULD NOT BELIEVE WHAT I JUST SAW, NOT even if you had seen it, too. I was outside, sprinkling salt on my driveway, a cold winter blast blowing through my coat, when my neighbor Curtis appeared from behind his house. ("Curtis, not Curt," he always says, and when you try to tease him about that he chases you with a pitchfork.) I was so stunned by what he was carrying I had to lean against my porch railing and catch my breath. No, it wasn't a lump of glowing nuclear waste or a baby hippo, although as weird as Curt (yes, Curt, just to tick him off) can be, neither would have surprised me. He carried a snow shovel.

This is shockingly epic, because I didn't think Curt even owned a snow shovel ... or a rake or a lawn mower or a garden hose. I didn't think Curt even knew how to use any of those yard implements. For that matter, I didn't think Curt could identify them if he saw them.

He's our obligatory strange neighbor. According to some unspoken cosmic law every neighborhood is required to have one. This is the person whose house you avoid by walking across the street; whose dog is usually a hulking, 200-pound mutant that accounts for the fact there are no small animals or young children on your block; and whose behavior is discussed in hushed tones during neighborhood events he is never invited to. This is Curt to a T, and we haven't even discussed his 1970s-era sideburns, those freaky aviator glasses, his oddly-stained undershirts or that prehistoric car he tools around in.

His neglected front yard looks like a massive fungal growth that could probably stand up and walk around. So for Curt to suddenly, inexplicably show an iota of concern for its appearance – or for that matter, concern for anything, including his own (ugh!) teeth – could very well portend the end of the world.

(No one knows what's in his backyard. One brave neighbor attempted five years ago to find out, and he was never seen again. We hold a candlelight vigil on the anniversary.)

Curt looks over at me with his one green and one blue eye – which never fail to give me the willies – and offers a barely discernible nod.

"Hey there, Curt - uh, Curtis," I say, and he stiffens and looks around for his pitchfork. "Gonna shovel the old walk, huh?" I've heard this guy speak on only two occasions: once when he called for his behemoth dog to let go of Mrs. Funderman from down the street, whom the beast dragged by her foot during his snack time; and once when a Girl Scout, whom all the neighbors tried frantically to wave away, knocked on his front door armed with a cookie order form. We all distinctly heard him growl, "Three hundred and twenty dozen Do-Si-Dos," but his sheer creepiness made the poor girl run right out of her shoes.

Curt hefts the shovel over his shoulder like a rifle during military drill, and heads for the curb. Just when I think he's going to defy all odds and actually clean his walkway, he rams the shovel into a large snowbank. That's when I notice a handmade sign taped to the handle:

> For Sale By Owner. $10
> FIRM and you MUST Shovel
> my Yard First.

"That will certainly get a lot of takers," I say, chuckling, but Curt isn't laughing. He gives me the once-over like a serial killer sizing up his next victim. Suddenly, his monster truck of a canine comes galloping from the back and halts in front of me, sniffing and drooling.

"Stop that," Curt orders. "It ain't snack time yet."

Even if it were, the only things that beast would get are the shoes I'm leaving behind.

Long, Blond Hairs

I HAVE THIS RUNNING JOKE WITH MY WIFE ABOUT long, blond hairs I keep finding on my computer keyboard at work. Well, the joke kind of runs with me more than it does with her. She doesn't know what to think of the long, blond hairs, and I don't know how to explain them. Now and again, one or two will appear across my computer keyboard, and, being the faithful, devoted husband I am I feel compelled to inform her. Nobody who works with me has long, blond hair, so that automatically ups the suspicion factor.

"Found another blond hair today," I tell her. "It was suddenly just there on the keyboard, lying diagonally across the letters X, D and R and the number five."

"Uh-huh," she says. I notice she isn't smiling, so I try levity.

"Must be the blond ghost again, heh heh," I say.

She doesn't get that humor, either. "Wish I knew where they were coming from," I continue cautiously. "How many people do you figure have long, blond hairs popping up on their keyboards? I mean, besides people with long, blond hair? You could probably count them on one hand. The people, I mean, not the blond hairs. You could probably count the blond hairs on my keyboard on four or five hands. Isn't that weird?"

We both realize I'm rambling, so I try a different tack. "Yeah, it's weird. But you wouldn't believe all the weird stuff that happens at work. The other day the copy machine attacked me. I was minding my own business, copying my latest disciplinary write-up for my personnel file, when the copier reached up and grabbed my shirt sleeve. Everybody came running when I started screaming, then somebody said, 'We should have known it was you' and yanked my sleeve loose. And now it has a toner stain."

"Uh-huh," she says.

"And this other time the break room microwave suddenly shorted out while I warmed up my wienerschnitzel."

"I'll just bet it did," she says. Her problem is, she overanalyzes everything. I mean everything, even a stray blond hair. I try to explain that not everything she encounters is flush with hidden meaning, but honestly, it's like living with Sigmund Freud.

"What does that mean?" she'll ask after I pay her a compliment.

"Just what I said," I'll reply. "That's some of the best chicken paprikas you've ever made."

"Some of the best," she'll repeat, frowning. "In other words, I've also made some bad paprikas." Her response can only lead to a very bad place, so I'll quickly resort to schmoozing. "You could never make bad paprikas, my sweet Pookie."

"But you said that's some of the best I've ever made. 'Some' implies not all, so what you're telling me is that some paprikas I've made wasn't good."

I'll start to sweat. "How did you get that from what I said? I never said some wasn't good. I said it was some of the best ..."

"I know what you said," she'll counter testily. "You said some of the best. If you look closely at the word 'some' it suggests there has been paprikas I've made in the past that didn't meet your lofty standards."

I'll try to defend myself, but "Whoa! Whoa!" is all I can manage, and I know her deep analysis of 'some' will never let me off the hook. So what chance do I have with a long, blond hair? None, I tell you. So next time one appears across my keyboard I'll keep quiet.

And from now on I'll use the word "all" around her, instead of "some." Although "all" implies the total amount, which suggests I mean all of something this time, which would mean I meant none of it previously. Which means I was never satisfied with something in the past.

Maybe I'll just sew my mouth shut.

Insufferable Language Snobs

My brown-eyed girl says I'm an insufferable English language snob. I'd take offense if she hadn't already accused me of a lot worse this week. For instance, she said I leave toenail clippings around the house. She said civilized people don't do that, so she would appreciate if I would stop acting like a Neanderthal and throw them away. I told her a Neanderthal wouldn't even know how to spell "toenail" or "clippings," so – HAH! – I'm already one step ahead of that evolutionary stage. I also asked her, if she thinks I'm such a Neanderthal, why I don't eat rodents, including their eyeballs and tails, and drag her around by her hair, to which she replied, "After I just washed it? You'd better not try!"

We have arguments like this because we're married. Arguments don't have to make perfect sense when you're married, because they're more about the husband trying vainly to prove for once that he's right. So you argue about toenail clippings, and which of you has the dumbest relatives, and where she ever got the idea that you like raspberry-scented shampoo. And the arguments get heated because she's got that smirk on her face that tells you you've already lost, since she's going to play dirty and bring up every stupid, insensitive thing you've ever said or done in the past, which, admittedly, could probably fill twenty of those college-ruled, five-subject notebooks.

She says I'm an insufferable English language snob because I have conniptions when people use words incorrectly. For instance, "I seen" or "He (she) don't," or "Their is my missing platypus." Or "Your welcome" or "me to." Spoken and written errors like those make me shudder, as they would any person who deals daily with words.

"Why do you let it bother you?" she asks. "Leave it alone."

But I can't. For instance, when I hear someone say "I seen" it makes my teeth hurt, like nails on a blackboard. I would never confront anyone with their mistake, especially the larger ones who look as though they could easily throw me for a touchdown pass, but just the same, I want to.

"Excuse me," I would say very politely, with a slight bow, "but I'm afraid you've expressed yourself incorrectly. For your edification, the proper way to say that is 'I saw,' not 'I seen.' Please also remember to write it that way from now on. Thank you so much for allowing me to offer this unsolicited, critical, and sanctimonious correction of what I consider your rather inferior use of English in front of everyone here. If your face is turning that daring shade of red, and you're using that most colorful language because I have embarrassed or angered you, why, that certainly was not my intention, although I will admit to it being a bonus. I would also appreciate it if you would put away that rather massive fist. Have a wonderful day."

I practiced that little speech on my wife to gauge whether or not she would consider it insulting, and she beaned me with a piece of sweet and sour pork (we were having dinner at the time, and watching *Jeopardy*! because, as she puts it, I'm a television snob as well).

"Are you trying to get beaten up?" she asked incredulously. "Why do you feel the need to be so pedantic? I mean, to who would you possibly say that to, anyway?"

"To whom," I corrected. More sweet and sour pork, an egg roll and a generous splash of duck sauce. Good thing I'm hungry for Chinese.

Toilet Bowls and Lady Ga Ga Fridays

STARING AT A BLANK PAGE DOESN'T GET THE JOB done. That's what a college journalism professor used to tell me. His deadline for a story would be practically sitting in my lap, and there I would be ... staring. I would be pumped up on caffeine and sugar, which had me dancing uncontrollably in my classroom seat, and yet my brain remained in neutral.

Oh, I'd be thinking various thoughts (Is it lunchtime yet? Why don't I look good in muscle shirts? Can I scratch myself there without anybody noticing?) but none of them related to my assignment. So I would continue staring.

"That's not getting the job done," the professor would say. He wore tight woolen suits and always had a toothpick jutting from the corner of his mouth. One time it stabbed his lip, and he actually cried and dabbed his eyes with a monogrammed hanky.

I knew staring at a blank page wouldn't get the job done, just like I knew I didn't have a shot with the girl sitting at the desk next to me, who wore form-fitting jeans and two-inch painted nails, and looked at me as if I were an incontinent, leprous troll. But I learned back then that writing is sometimes like trying to stuff a grumpy grizzly bear into a test tube – futile and agonizing.

It's the same where I work now. Once a week I'm supposed to be clever and hilarious, and don't think my boss doesn't hold me to that standard. He'll strut over to my desk with that no-nonsense, authoritative look on his face – the one that reminds me of a constipated bulldog – and ask if I'm feeling funny today, "because, mister, judging from the last couple of pieces you've written you couldn't win honorable mention in a bad joke contest." He calls me "mister" when he's fed up, which is often enough that everyone in the office thinks that's my real name.

While he studies my employment contract, looking for loopholes, I concentrate harder on the blank page in front of me and wonder ... *Have I worn this shirt twice this week? I wonder if someone will loan me five dollars? Who keeps flicking rubber bands at my head? Why did I ever choose writing as a profession*. It couldn't have been for money or glitz. And I know it wasn't for the perks here, which, if I count carefully, have amounted to three. They include a subscription to the Toilet Bowl Cleaner of the Month Club and mandatory Dress Like Lady Ga Ga Fridays, which aren't as bad as they sound if you have nice legs.

No, I think I chose writing because it gave me a platform to express my innermost thoughts and feelings. It also saved me from continuing a hellacious stint as a bill collector, which consisted of receiving threats on my life, imaginative name-calling and suggestions of self-maiming that probably aren't physically possible unless you're a contortionist.

So I sit here, staring and staring, and I finally turn to a co-worker who recently felt the need to move his desk a few feet further away from mine, and reposition his chair with its back to me. I ask if he has any good ideas, and he suggests I do a piece on the fact that I still owe him three dollars for my share of a pizza lunch everybody kicked in four – no, FIVE! – months ago, and another twenty dollars for the bet I lost over how many pennies he could fit into his unusually large and deep bellybutton.

So I turn to another co-worker, who says she has nothing to say to me until I stop rummaging through her bottom desk drawer and swiping her mini powdered doughnuts.

Finally. I turn in desperation to my boss, who is whooping because he thinks he found a loophole in my contract, which means I may not have to be funny after all.

Thank goodness, because I've run out of bad jokes.

I Like Africa Hot

STIFLING HEAT SO FAR THIS SUMMER HAS BEEN amazing. To me, anyway. I step onto my front porch and feel the relentless sun and blast of hot air and sigh, "Aaaaah!" with gusto, and Mike three doors down hears me and throws a large tuft of his burnt-out lawn in my direction.

Mike's the guy whose lawn you have to beat each summer; it's always plush, and a luxurious shade of green, and if he spies a weed horning in he'll strap a huge tank to his back containing a pesticide all his neighbors suspect is not FDA-approved. Every time he sprays it everybody within a two-block radius, including squirrels, suddenly lapses into temporary amnesia and gets sleepy enough to lie down and nap right where they are. Believe you me, that can be risky when you're on a ladder removing a wasps' nest.

Mike has tried everything this summer to get his turf to jump up and boogie, including performing what he insists is a genuine tribal rain dance that involves a lot of grunting and stomping in a circle with his arms flailing at the sky. Mike tends to prove a lot that he is slightly unbalanced. Anyway, with precipitation holding steady at minus six billion percent even the dance hasn't worked, and his grass just keeps getting browner, so he doesn't appreciate a good "Ahhhh!" from a fan of hot weather.

"Come over here and say that!" he dares me. I'm tempted, but he's wearing saggy Bermuda shorts with knee-high black socks and penny loafers, and that old sailor's cap that makes him look like Thurston Howell III, so I think he's feeling less stable than usual and I'm not looking for trouble.

He sneers when I decline his offer, and kicks angrily at a dandelion that had the unmitigated gall to grow on his property. He stomps toward his garage, so I know the tank of questionable pesticide is coming out, and I go in and lie down on the couch for my nap, which is way better than on the rose bush in my yard like the last time he sprayed.

To paraphrase an old movie, it's been Africa hot, which you can tell by the way Ollie down at the corner sprawls on his porch furniture in just a pair of form-fitting, lime-green swimming trunks, with a beer cooler at his feet and a battery-operated mini-fan hanging from a cord around his neck. He lazily swats at the occasional fly, frequently sips at his drink and complains to his dog, Chester, that if he had the sense God gave penguins he would be lying with the lid closed in the portable freezer in his garage. Ollie shouldn't legally be allowed to wear those teensy swimming trunks for any reason, but you have to forgive him during this humid, sticky weather.

Although it's not the majority opinion, I like Africa hot. Africa hot sucks all the energy out of your body and leaves you wilted and good for nothing but sprawling around like Ollie and continuously hydrating. It's a great excuse not to perform household chores or do yard work. You give your spouse a look of pure exhaustion and dramatically fan yourself with her *In Touch* magazine, and say, "I'll get working on the laundry just as soon as it cools off," which isn't fooling her, because the air-conditioning is on full blast. She's cleaning the kitchen and shooting murderous looks in your direction while you sprawl with your third frosty adult beverage in the past hour, so you know your sloth can't last much longer But to prolong it just a little longer you sigh and wipe nonexistent sweat off your forehead and moan, "It's Africa hot."

She should be grateful to have me. In a parallel universe she's probably married to Ollie and dealing with those lime-green trunks.

Obligation to Feel Obligated

I HATE NEW YEAR'S RESOLUTIONS BECAUSE THEY obligate you to be better. Not saying I don't want to be better, but I don't like the obligation part. Ever since I was young I have abhorred being obligated to anything, and I have only my Catholic upbringing to blame. You see, I was an altar boy during my formative years, which required serving Mass at very inopportune times. There I would be during a summer evening, running free and loose with my neighborhood pals, going to Alma's Market around the corner for an orange sherbet Push-Up, which you couldn't do better than on a hot, sticky day, and then my mother would send a brother or sister to fetch me. I would know exactly what that meant, and my heart would freeze: She had volunteered me again for duty.

What would happen is, some other altar boy assigned to the daily 7:30 p.m. Mass at church would also be enjoying a Push-Up with his buddies and decide he didn't want to interrupt his summertime bliss. So he would go to his mother, complaining and holding his stomach, claiming the treat he just ate must have been tainted, because – seriously, Mom! – he was going to lose his cookies if he didn't relax on the couch right away and watch television the rest of the night. He would be so convincing that his mother would call my mother, her church friend, and ask if I couldn't possibly take her son's place, since he was at death's door, watching *Match Game.*

So I'd have to clean up and scoot into good clothes and run the three blocks to the church in my uncomfortable patent leather shoes to get there on time, while my mother interrupted my complaining with, "Jesus sacrificed for you, so you can do the same for Him!"

This happened often enough, and also for the 5:30 a.m. Mass (always in the dead of winter when I was buried comfortably in my blanket), that I learned to hate being obligated, especially by somebody else. The tradition was continued briefly by my brown-eyed girl ("I'm sure when David gets home from a long work day he would LOVE to immediately jump back into the car and spend five hours transporting pies and cakes all over town for your garden club fundraiser!") until I forever put the kibosh on that by learning to whine about it in a horrific pitch just below what only dogs can hear.

Now comes New Year's, and she has subtly reminded me that I can really afford to improve upon myself, especially my morning sessions in the bathroom, which leave her contemplating divorce more often than they should. To be fair, she says, she'll make some resolutions, too, although, obviously, they won't have to be nearly as extreme as mine.

So I balk, reminding her of my intense dislike for being obligated, and telling her I should be the judge of what needs improving. Well, that starts another discussion I don't want to be obligated to, so I tell her I'm cramping from a tainted Push-Up I just ate (not even bothering to Google "Push-Up" first, to check whether they're still made) and need to lie down immediately and watch TV all night or I'm going to lose my cookies. She hands me a bucket and says, "Cheers" before re-launching into her myriad reasons why I should never attempt to be the judge of anything – "Good gravy, wouldn't that be a disaster!" – and that, frankly, she's been praying for New Year's resolution time so I would finally have no excuse not to straighten up.

So Happy New Year, everyone, and I just made a resolution not to make any more resolutions, and that was greeted with as much enthusiasm as cooties in your underpants. So here comes yet another unwanted discussion, and now I think I really am about to go cookie-less.

Teenagers and Christmas Gifts

THE 16-YEAR-OLD PAUSES WHILE PREPARING HIS Christmas list and asks us how much money we have. I open my wallet and expose two forlorn dollar bills. My wife leans over and plucks one of them for herself.

"Where's the rest of it?" he asks. We look at him and laugh, because that really is a good one. He doesn't realize the rest of it is sheltering, warming, feeding, clothing and generally paying for him and his brother.

"Because," he continues, "the stuff I want for Christmas costs a lot more than two dollars."

"Mine, too," I tell him. "Good luck to both of us." It used to be easier when they were younger, and the cost of their toys didn't rival the national debt. If we told them the knock-off version we bought them of the pricey toy they absolutely had to have was just as good, they believed us. If we shopped at a dollar store, they had no clue. We could usually finance the Christmas season by only occasionally selling the stray body organ.

Now the 16-year-old comes to us and says hesitantly, "I think you'll think what I want for Christmas is too expensive." Red flags sprout from our heads and start waving vigorously. "Why do you say that?" I ask.

"Because what I want for Christmas is too expensive," he replies.

"But you're going to ask for it anyway."

"It's the only thing I want. You don't have to buy me another present for the rest of my life."

"You said that last Christmas."

"But this is different. This is epic. Look."

He shows us an electronic gadget on a catalog page. The price almost makes me swallow my tongue.

"I really, really want it," he pleads. "It would make me so happy that I'd probably start actually listening to you and doing what you tell me the very nanosecond you say to do it. Wouldn't that be awesome?"

"Why can't you do that now?" I ask.

"Because I'm an unhappy teenager without this," he says, pointing to the gadget.

He's always been a drama king, but even he must know this is laying it on a bit thick.

"Pocky's parents are getting him one," he advises us.

Now I smell a rat. Whenever this boy wants something he tells us with a guileless face that his friend Pocky is getting one. It's his idea of cleverly planting guilt in us, although I'm sure after Pocky showed his parents the catalog page they tried not to swallow their tongues, too.

"I just don't know," I say. "Mom and I will have to talk about it."

He sprawls on the couch. "Go ahead. I'll wait."

"In private," I tell him.

"Pocky's mom and dad talk about everything right in front of him," he says. Which explains so much about Pocky, who I personally believe would benefit greatly from electroshock therapy, or at the very least a good multivitamin.

Later, his mother and I agree the 16-year-old's Christmas wish is pricey but manageable if I sell my feet on the black market. But that obligates us to buy his brothers gifts of equal value, which means also giving up a kidney, and possibly a lung.

"If this keeps up every year, all I'll have left is my stomach and some ear wax," I tell her.

"Yeah, I'd just as soon you sell the ear wax too," she says.

That isn't going to happen. I use it when I run out of gum.

Bunch of Worthless Hairballs

FIVE CATS LIVE IN MY HOUSE. I FIND THIS FACT especially funny in light of the intruder who broke in last week, helped himself to a meal in our bread drawer and vanished without a trace. My brown-eyed girl startled me from a nap to announce this crime with barely-contained panic: "We have a mouse!" With five cats living in my house.

During times of hardship and crises over the years, we always comforted ourselves by lovingly stroking their fur and saying, "At the very least, we'll never have mice."

I barged through the house, looking for our feline hit squad. I found all five members stretched out on our bed. One was snoring louder than my wife, a real accomplishment.

"Hey!" I yelled at them, "We have a mouse!" Three of them yawned, stretched languorously and looked at me, befuddled. The other two didn't even roll over. "We have a mouse!" I repeated. "Code One! Up and at 'em!" The largest cat, an orange monstrosity who wouldn't leave a warm bed during a full-scale nuclear attack, blinked sleepily and looked at me as if I were insane. His father, a skittish gray behemoth who would run from a housefly, began what appeared to be a long, luxurious bath. The third one I managed to rouse, the temperamental mother and wife, respectively, of the first two, decided she wasn't interested and plopped her head back down.

"Come on!" I protested. "Earn your kitty litter! Go get it!"

Nothing.

I pointed toward the open bedroom door. "Attack!" The father and son looked at each other, confused.

"Hey, you mental giants, go get the MOUSE!" That outburst woke up one of the two remaining cats. She rolled onto her back, hoping for a belly rub. The three I had already awakened watched her and followed suit. "Are you kidding me?" I bellowed.

But they're not. They're so fat, so pampered, so ultimately spoiled I'm surprised they would recognize a mouse, let alone know what to do with one.

"Wait a minute. Didn't you say one of these lazy lumps is a real mouser?" I asked my wife. "You're always going on about what a good mouser she'd be." My wife pointed to the one who hadn't stirred since I charged into the room.

"Hey, you! Rip Van Winkle. Wake up!" I shouted. The calico's furry little head stirred a moment, then she rolled around slowly to reveal droopy eyes. The mouse was asleep in her fur.

"GET IT!" I screamed, and suddenly my wife was on top of her chest of drawers and all the cats, including the one with the mouse clinging to it, were on their feet, searching wildly for their target.

"RIGHT THERE!" I yelled, pointing to the mouse, which was looking around as well. But they're so ignorant they all dived off the bed and started running helter-skelter, looking for the mouse. The mouse, which broke loose from the mouser during the dive, was running with the cats, looking for itself.

I grabbed an empty jar from the kitchen and held it upside down over the mouse after it finally pooped out. The cats kept running in circles, but each one stopped momentarily to peer quizzically through the jar at the stranger before resuming their chase for it.

There are going to be repercussions. I am not going to tolerate a bunch of worthless hairballs who don't earn their keep. I'm putting my foot down, just as soon as I can wake them all back up. The mouse, too.

Poor Man's Steak

IT HAS TAKEN ALMOST ELEVEN YEARS, ONE WIFE and three kids, but I have finally realized what my primary duty is in this household: Stay out of trouble. And you'd think that would be easy, wouldn't you?

"What did you do with the leftover chicken?" my brown-eyed girl asks accusingly. When I was a longtime bachelor I never would have asked myself that, just patted my stomach and looked for dessert. However, I'm standing before my personal judge and jury, so I have to tread very carefully.

"Uh...nothing?" I lie, but she's so much smarter than me it's not worth my breath to say it.

"I told you I was going to use it to make dinner tonight," she says. "I said, 'Don't eat the leftover chicken, I'm going to use it to make dinner tonight.' It's such a simple statement. Clear, and to the point."

"And you did say it forcefully," I concede. "You even emphasized 'don't.'"

"So where is the chicken?" she asks, hands on hips, a sign if there ever was one that responding, "Crossing the road" would be funny only to me.

"Uh ... " I say again, trying to remember which of my

standard excuses for poor husbandship (yes, I made that word up) I have used the least number of times this month.

"Do you know of any way I can make chicken a la king without chicken?"

I do, in fact, because when you're a single guy making your own meals you learn to be innovative, so the grilled cheese and peanut butter aren't always the same. But it's been through trial and oh-so-much error that I have learned that angry questions like this a la king one my wife just fired at me are meant to be rhetorical, and showing off with alternative recipes involving beer and gooey gobs of cheese will only turn her annoyed shade of red even redder. And if she gets any redder our marriage license will probably burst into flames.

"Uh ... " I stammer again, because it's only dumb or inexperienced husbands who don't continue with "uh" when it seems to be working really well for them.

"What do you suggest we have for dinner?"

Well, I have some really freaky grilled cheese and peanut butter ideas, I think.

"Tell you what," she says. "How about you go make us something? And no grilled cheese or peanut butter."

She actually wants me to cook? She must be as desperate as she is angry.

"Sure," I say enthusiastically while trying to actually look enthusiastic. "What ingredients do we have?"

"Not chicken," she says, lobbing a final grenade in my direction.

"Good one," I say, chuckling, but stop because the look on her face could melt cast iron. So I whip up poor man's steak, a basic recipe involving hamburger, and the only one my mother sent with me when I moved out. It's a recipe to this day she insists didn't suggest her doubt in my ability to succeed. The meal comes out of the oven a bit singed after I become engrossed in a TV show about mental focus and forget to check it, but with a lot of ketchup and a pinched nose it isn't bad.

The leftovers – lots of them – are in the refrigerator, and I'm not about to touch them. My wife assured me it would be a blessing if I ate all of them, that she and the boys wouldn't be the least bit upset, but after the chicken fiasco I'm not about to fall for that. I don't care how red her face is getting because I'm refusing.

She's stuck with me, even if our marriage license does burst into flames.

The Old-fashioned Candy Counter

ALMA SAT BEHIND THE COUNTER ON HER STOOL, reading the latest celebrity gossip rag as we pressed our noses up against the glass.

"Stop that! You're gonna smudge!" she said. But it was hard not to, with all those goodies beckoning us at her candy counter. Alma owned the carryout around the corner from our house, and it was Saturday, or as we called it, Spend Day. My brothers and sisters and I scooted to her small store almost the minute our dad dropped our allowances in our hands.

We each got a dime, not much by standards even way back then, but enough to buy us something sweet. I earned mine in part by taking my turn at washing the dinner dishes one night a week. Cleaning the dishes of twelve people is no small feat for anyone, and especially when you had brothers who would deliberately make such a gross mess of their plates, silverware and glasses that scrubbing them chained you to the kitchen sink half the night. And there always was a greasy, caked-on pan the meat was cooked in that I would vigorously attack with steel wool and half a bottle of dish soap, spraying sudsy water until my mother would say, "That's enough! You just have to clean it, not kill it!"

I also had to sweep the front porch each Saturday morning, another frustrating chore when my cartoons were on and I couldn't watch them. My work would fall under the inspecting eye of my dad, who wasn't about to give up a dime for a sloppy, half-hearted attempt. "You can do better than that," he would admonish. I'd offer excuses with a teary, fatigued look, but giving my dad excuses was like giving Mighty Mouse a dirt bike. (That comparison somehow made perfect sense in my head, so I'm going with it.)

I would pout for five minutes, and when that didn't work I would do the job correctly and receive my dime, which would burn a hole the size of Brazil in my pocket. Then I would scoot with my siblings over to Alma's store and do my part to smudge the glass, which always made Alma sigh and break out the cleaner. It was an old-fashioned candy counter, with penny items on the top shelf, five-cent items below that, then ten-cent items and, on the bottom shelf, the coveted quarter and fifty-cent treasures.

My eyes always drifted to that bottom shelf, to a display of drawstring pouches bulging with bubble gum pieces shaped and colored like gold nuggets. They cost a quarter, which to a lower middle class boy like me might as well have been a million dollars. With his dime my brother always got penny candy, like strips of candy buttons or tiny wax bottles with flavored syrup in them. My sister would buy the foot-long roll of gum and slowly portion it out to herself over the next week. But I wanted the ersatz gold nuggets, and if I would just resolve to save my dimes for three weeks I could have them.

You may as well have asked me to croon love ballads to Katie Felder, who was my secret crush at school. Three weeks to a kid is an eternity; the world could end before then or, worse yet, Alma could run out of candy. So I always spent my dime on a pack of collectible cards that included a stale stick of gum or on a multi-colored coconut bar, then mooned again the next week over the pouches of gold.

I told my brown-eyed girl about this once, and we laughed over my inability back then to save. Now the 16-year-old has bopped into the room carrying store bags holding a computer game and magic cards.

"How much of your birthday money do you have left?" my wife asks warily.

"None!" he says happily.

"You didn't think to save any?"

"I was going to, so I can buy a car," he says, "but that will take too long. So I got this stuff."

He and I are going to have a talk about this. And I think it's going to include a story about twenty-five cents worth of gum.

Teenagers: They Keep the Cupboard Bare

NO ONE KNOWS WHAT HAPPENED TO THE PEOple from the abandoned 19th Century merchant ship *Mary Celeste* or from the deserted colony of Roanoke in 1590 in what is now North Carolina. The same goes for the fates of New York City Judge Joseph Crater in 1930, and legendary pilot Amelia Earhart. They all simply vanished, never to be found.

The same vanishing act occurs daily with food in my house, but it's not so mysterious. We have two teenagers. I sat watching television as the 15-year-old walked into the kitchen. For the next half-hour I listened as the refrigerator and cupboard doors kept opening and closing, the microwave kept running, delicious aromas kept wafting and dirty dishes kept piling in the sink. Afterward he strolled away nonchalantly.

Don't go in there, I kept telling myself. Resist temptation and don't go in there to check on how many groceries are left. Just console yourself with the fact that if he left behind even two slices of processed cheese and a grape you should count yourself lucky.

My brown-eyed girl drifted into the kitchen, then staggered out looking pale. "What happened in there?" she asked.

"Need you ask?" I replied.

"That's impossible," she said. "He could not possibly have eaten all of that. A stomach can't take that much abuse."

"He doesn't look at it as abuse. He looks at it as lunch." I remember this kid when he was a preschooler who fought his mother and me at every meal. "How many more bites do I have to take?" became his official battle cry, and no matter how many we instructed he would take an eternity to finish them.

Now we're the ones asking anxiously, "How many more bites are you going to take?" as he devours one food item after another, plowing through our grocery supply like a swarm of ravenous locusts. "I'm still hungry," he'll reply, and to keep up with the demand I'll immediately begin the search for a second and third job, or, if no employment is available, plans to knock over a bank.

Half an hour after a trip to replenish our stock he announces, "We're out of bread, milk, eggs, canned stuff and snacks. But the good news is, I'm feeling full – for now."

We have thought about charging him for meals, but even Bill Gates would go broke financing this boy's appetite. So in a moment of panic I blatantly lied by suggesting he looks fat and needs to diet.

"Don't say that," my wife complained. "You'll damage his self-esteem."

"Don't worry about his self-esteem. He probably ate that, too," I said drily. Our middle child, whom we occasionally spot outside his room when the moon is full, has a stealthier approach to ransacking our food but inflicts no less damage. We never see him strike, and proof of his food raids are better hidden. Often, it's just a feeling.

"He's been here," my wife whispered as the hair on her neck stood up. "I can sense it."

We were examining the kitchen, yet nothing looked amiss. "Check the cupboards," she said.

I cautiously approached the one nearest me, took a deep breath, then flung it open.

"AAAUUUGGH!" my wife shrieked, her entire head of hair jolting. There it was, a huge gap on the shelves where food used to be. "Saints preserve us, he picked us cleaned!" she cried.

In a desperate attempt to thwart them both we resorted to piling all the remaining food in a corner and camouflaging it to look like a smelly, revolting garbage pile. The plan backfired. They both thought it was their bedroom.

A Dead Horse in the Plumbing

PLUMBING IS NOT SOMETHING I'M ORDINARILY interested in. It's there, it works, and I pour store-bought toxic chemicals down household drains to melt the occasional clog.

That didn't work this time. As I was lathering up in the shower I thought I heard a repeated glurp. I wasn't certain, because I had been singing *How Am I Supposed To Live Without You?* It's one of the smarmiest, most maudlin, tear-jerking songs ever written, and I was singing it soulfully and as closely to on-key as was possible. I enjoy loudly singing smarmy, maudlin songs in the shower, which is why, after numerous complaints within our zip code, my brown-eyed girl had the bathroom sound-proofed.

I was just getting to the part in the song where I ask my departing lover how I'm supposed to carry on, which always causes the slightest hitch in my throat, when I thought I heard the glurping outside the shower. Glurps are not too common at my house, unless you want to count the 15-year-old's infamous belches, and those are more of a glorified glorp. So when I thought I heard a second glurp, and then a third, I forgot all about carrying on after an ignoramus lover ditched me, and turned off the shower.

It was coming from the toilet, and from the drain of our separate bathtub. Even someone as poorly versed in household maintenance as me knows that isn't correct plumbing etiquette. Toilets and drains are not supposed to talk to you unless you're a member of the Addams family, or are deluded enough to think you are.

I left the shower and stood dripping in front of the toilet, examining it as though I were a plumbing guru, which anyone can tell you I'm the farthest thing from. It didn't look the least bit sick, so I flushed it to make certain. The water rose like the biblical flood. At the same time water bubbled out of the bathtub drain, and I shrieked like a banshee in labor.

That was a week ago. Since then, two guys who looked like they knew all about the business end of a plumber's snake came knocking. "Nothing to it," they said. "We'll have you back in business in five minutes." More than two hours later they were both covered in glop, which is typical for plumbers dealing with the glurp, and both were shaking their heads incredulously. Worst case they'd ever seen, they said. Couldn't be any worse if we had plugged the pipes with a dead horse, which, they weren't so certain we hadn't.

I simply love to hear such an inviting diagnosis. It makes me harken back to the excitement of purchasing our home, when my wife and I were so wide-eyed, or in such complete denial, we couldn't imagine anything going wrong with our castle. It was a wonderful feeling, even if it was three spongy porch steps, two broken cupboard doors and one sputtering refrigerator ago.

So then, instead of two guys and a plumber's snake, we had what seemed like thirteen guys in muddy boots clomping back and forth inside and outside of our house, faces grim, saying ominous things like, "Looks like we're going to have to tear it all out." and warning us the smell could possibly knock us unconscious. It seemed to go on forever, until they finally assured us everything should be better.

That was five days ago. I was in the shower the other day, singing *When A Man Loves A Woman* (although not the horrible Michael Bolton version) when I thought I heard a glurp. I stepped out, flushed the toilet, watched water gush frighteningly into the bowl and shrieked like a banshee in labor.

If it is a dead horse in the pipes we'll just move. There's no sense beating it.

They Don't Make Parents Like they Used to

PARENTS AREN'T LIKE THEY WERE WHEN I WAS A kid. I can remember getting into trouble at home and trying not to hyperventilate while waiting for the other shoe to drop. Just knowing I would have to face my dad was enough to make me squeeze my eyes shut and pray for a killer bolt of lightning, or that a lion would suddenly escape the zoo and swallow me whole.

My dad was not the type to sit you down, stroke your hair and ask gently why you did what you did. He would come home exhausted from eight hours of factory work feeling hungry and a little ticked off at his supervisor. And there you would be, wide-eyed and trembling as my mother described to him how you made your younger sister eat an earthworm, omitting the part where you considerately let her dunk it in Nestle's Quik first, an act of kindness you hoped would cut you some slack.

Never one to mince words, or even use them if he had to, my dad would dispense justice, usually in the form of a spanking, and you would walk away stinging and wiser for the experience. He was fair but no-nonsense, and when he said something you knew he meant it.

I never looked at my dad as a buddy; he was the authority in our house, the final word, the wisdom and the provider. There was never any doubt he knew his role and took it to heart. He was raised in a generation of men who never shirked from their role to lead.

My mother was the same, maybe gentler in her authoritative role but insistent on good behavior and following a moral and ethical code. Rules could be strict, expectations were clear, and inappropriate behavior was addressed. She was Mom, and disrespecting her was absolutely verboten, lest you wanted to face my dad's considerable wrath.

These days I see a lot of men and women who simply refuse to grow up. They reach adulthood, experience the accompanying necessities of propriety and responsibility, decide they don't like the taste and choose to remain perpetually fifteen. Consequently, their children are raised essentially by larger versions of themselves: self-centered, emotionally immature parents whose stunted values, continued juvenile behavior and carelessly-displayed bad habits are passed on to the next generation.

If I had ever sworn at or in front of my parents ... If I had ever called them names or blatantly flouted their rules ... If I had ever told them to shut up, or something worse ... The fact is, I never would have. There was no question they were parents, and simply by virtue of their responsible actions and deeds they demanded respect and obedience. If I strayed – and being a child I most certainly did – I was quickly and firmly put back in my place. There was no question who was in charge, or what would happen if I challenged that authority.

The other day I watched a mom in the throes of irritation drop the F-bomb on her pre-adolescent child and throw a temper tantrum in the middle of a department store. The child responded in kind.

That would have never happened in my family. Thank God.

Family Dining without Bloodshed

RECENTLY, I LUNCHED WITH CO-WORKERS IN A restaurant that provided cloth napkins. Those things make me uncomfortable. I always imagine the thoughts of the poor schmuck who will have to wash mine afterward: Yuck! Just give him a trough, why dontcha?

I grew up using mostly paper napkins and plates. My frazzled parents didn't have the time or money to fool with fancy table implements, and we kids didn't have much opportunity or the upper-crust breeding to use them.

In my neighborhood, a fork was a fork, a spoon a spoon and a knife a knife. They were all the same size and shape, and you got one of each. There was none of this messing with a salad type and a soup type, or wondering which one to use during which course. Our silverware came in a discounted cardboard box, a 58-piece set of basic stainless steel cutlery for about five dollars including sales tax.

Believe me, you didn't want anything fancier in a house with ten kids, where meals often resembled feeding frenzies among sharks. After we properly thanked God for our bounty the tabletop would be a blur of arms and grubby hands snatching at the mountain of dinner rolls, the pounds of string beans and the standard 50-gallon vat of mashed potatoes required for a family of twelve. My father would serve and slice the meat with the caution of someone feeding piranha, always careful to avoid the slashing teeth.

My mother would sit, exhausted from hours of cooking, only to see every crumb sucked up within milliseconds into the black holes that were our mouths. "Slow down and chew your food," she'd say, wagging her finger at us from waist level. She didn't dare wag it any higher for fear it would get caught in the cross-sucking inhaling action around the table and she would be pulled down somebody's throat.

There wasn't much in the way of conversation. My parents always attempted to initiate simulating dinner talk with questions like, "Who stole the pork chop off my plate?" and, "Why is there a bite out of the tablecloth?" Our responses always came in the form of lip-smacking, elbow-bumping and repetitive, annoying table-leg kicking that raised my parents' blood pressure to dangerous levels.

It was considered good table etiquette in our family if everyone walked away from a meal with all of their fingers intact.

Because the table seated only eight, the four youngest kids were relegated to some outdated kiddie desks bought from our elementary school and lined up against the far dining room wall. Their old-fashioned drawers were perfect places to ditch any part of the meal we didn't like. Weeks later, my mother would discover dried-out carrots and hot dogs so petrified you couldn't split them with a diamond cutter.

Of course, on holidays and other special occasions, my mother would bring out the nice matching plates and glasses. These weren't the everyday plastic ones accumulated from thirty-seven different family-style collections which were a jumble of shapes and sizes and had cartoon characters printed all over them.

And when I say the good stuff matched, I don't mean that everything matched exactly. With ten kids in the house breaking anything that wasn't nailed down, she had salvaged three very nice patterned dishes from a set she bought twelve years ago, and two more that survived the cute set from five years ago, plus a couple of glasses from another set she had purchased last year, etc. When each set had been brand-new, she had presented us with the same warning: "These are my good dishes. You kids had better take care of them!" (SMASH!).

It was a challenge to dine at our house during holidays. All the different patterns lining the table could make you too dizzy to eat.

When my father retired from his job, the company presented him with a gorgeous set of golden cutlery lined in a heavy wooden box and cushioned with velvety red cloth. He raised the lid to a chorus of Oooo! and Ahhh! and when my brother reached out to touch those beauties Dad practically slammed the lid down on his knuckles.

"Nobody touches these," he growled. "They're going to stay nice and unscratched and unbent. Now everyone close your eyes, so I can hide them where no one will ever find them."

These days, I open my own kitchen cabinet at dinnertime and pull out paper plates which are thin as tissue paper and come in a package of 20,000. I reach into another cabinet and pull out oversized souvenir plastic tumblers from an amusement park that must be held with two hands and easily hold a gallon of liquid. Then I pull open the silverware drawer and withdraw what resembled eating utensils before the kids used them repeatedly as makeshift tools.

I set the table, and the boys clamor into the room and slide into their seats, salivating and complaining that they're starving because they haven't had anything to eat in fifteen whole minutes. As we say grace, all of them start kicking the table legs.

Dancing to the Beat of Her Heart

MY DAD WAS SO SMOOTH ON THE DANCE FLOOR. As a child, I would watch him glide effortlessly with my mother in his arms, around and around. He put his own deft touch on a basic two-step, a lilt in his footwork that made him look debonair. After years of tripping the light fantastic together they were perfectly in sync, our own Fred and Ginger, and watching them always made me feel happy and secure.

I wish I had it – that airy spring in the feet, that graceful spin. The way he would softly clutch my mother's hand, the other firmly around her waist, and guide her through a gentle ballet.

Unfortunately, I'm a cliché. As a single man, dancing with women always carried a touch of embarrassment. I used a simple box-step my older sister taught me before my first high school dance. As we practiced, I knew she had inherited Dad's grace and fluid movement. I tried awkwardly to keep up, my feet a tangle, my rhythm incomprehensible.

Fast-dancing was probably worse. I always fortified myself with several adult beverages before skulking with my wary partner deep into the center of the crowd. Those around me would sway and bend to the music like regulars on *Dance Fever.* I flailed my arms and contorted grotesquely, thankful that no one seated at tables surrounding the dance floor could see me.

Some men are naturals. They are the elite, those who, for reasons unclear, were granted the gift. All of my life I have watched them – always with a sense of awe and a tingle of jealousy – as they move deftly, effortlessly. They are John Travolta in *Saturday Night Fever* and Sean Patrick Thomas in *Save the Last Dance*, swinging their hips and arms in perfect time and creating magic to a pulsing beat.

With the passage of time, I am losing whatever trace of lightness and agility I might possess. Watching me today on the dance floor is akin to watching someone trying desperately to stay on his feet during an earthquake.

So during a quiet moment at home, when everyone's attention is occupied elsewhere, I slip into the bathroom and examine myself in the mirror. Middle age hasn't so much crept into my life as brazenly pushed its way through the door. I look at the paunch and the thin hair, and I know that any dash I may have once had is buried somewhere beneath my slight double chin.

Regardless, I do a brief shimmy to loosen my joints, then start a simple dance step that won't injure me too severely. I play a favorite tune repeatedly in my head as I bump and boogie, noticing my stiff movements and wild gestures, wondering why I wasn't rewarded with the touch.

As I attempt a complicated pivot and spin, I see my beloved off to the side, watching quietly. I stop and turn to face her, waiting for the inevitable laughter, the sly comment. I have certainly made a fool of myself in front of her before, but not in this way. Dancing has always been my Achilles Heel, something I find difficult to share even with her.

"No, Keep going," she says. I feel the crimson rising in my cheeks, and begin to walk past her, but she stops me. "No, really, I want to see more."

"Don't," I tell her. "You've seen more than enough."

She smiles. "You're not bad. I mean, really, not bad. Come on."

She is a goddess on the dance floor. Whether fast or slow, watching her is a feast for the eyes. Moving with her to music, I've always felt like a trained bear.

She turns on the radio. A song I've always loved fills the air.

"Come on," she says encouragingly. "Let's dance. Just you and me."

I protest, but her brown eyes are warm and sincere. Grudgingly, I begin to shake and rattle, bend and sway. As she grins and nods I gain confidence, trying hard to imitate her style and her incredible moves. It's different with her. I'm not blushing.

The tune changes to something slow and seductive. She pulls me into her arms, rests her head against me and we move gracefully, in tandem. It's my simple box-step, but the moment is heavenly and she's moving like an angel, so I attempt a bit of my dad's flair.

"You're a natural," she lies lovingly, and I pull her tighter.

When I look up, the boys are standing there, smiling. They look happy and secure.

May the Good Saints Preserve Me

IT'S FIVE-THIRTY ON A COLD WINTER MORNING. My dad wakes me and says to shake a leg. He calls me twice more before I manage to roll out of my warm bed. Sometimes, it's tough being Catholic.

A half-hour later he drops me off at church. I'm grumbling, because I'm sure not even God is awake yet. And even if He is, He's probably still in bed, in a comfy robe sipping decaf and watching cartoons before taking on the world.

I'm eleven years old, and have early-bird altar boy duty. It's the first Mass of the day. The only people who ever attend it are two ancient babushkas and, occasionally, the church maintenance man if he's replacing a light bulb nearby.

It's the worst of the altar boy gigs. Your Lucky Charms are still sloshing in your stomach, you could find only socks with holes at the toes, and now you have to perform the service while half-asleep.

This duty wasn't my idea. I was perfectly content being a typical fifth-grader. But my older brother had been an altar boy, and my mother was strongly convinced the experience had made him a more spiritual, well-rounded person. This, despite the fact that he spent more time in the principal's office than the principal. Now she has decided the baton will be passed to me.

I shouldn't gripe. This is what you do when you're a nice Catholic boy, and it impresses nice Catholic girls. It's just this early morning business, and those services in the early evening during summer vacation when, as much as you love and want to serve your creator, you'd rather be home having a water balloon fight.

Prior to showtime I help the old priest put on his vestments, which can be dicey because he's fussy and impatient. ("Oh, for the love of everything sacred! Go get the lint brush!") I also prepare the cruet holding the sacramental wine, careful to fill it extra high so that later the other altar boy and I can cop a couple swigs before returning it.

My other job is to light altar candles that are taller than the Empire State Building. This is supposed to be accomplished by raising up a long, golden rod with a lighted wick on one end. But I'm four-foot-nothing, and the candle tops are hovering in the stratosphere. The only way I'll manage to light those babies is by holding a torch while hanging from a low-flying aircraft.

One of the babushkas is kneeling up front, kneading a huge rosary she could use for a lasso. When she sees my predicament she mutters, "Oh, for the love of everything sacred!" in Polish and swats the dozing maintenance man in the pew behind her. "Be useful, and go help da boy!" she growls.

After that humiliation I go to dress in a cassock and surplice – a long, black robe and a billowy white tunic that fits over the robe. They seem to come in all sizes but mine. The clock is ticking, so after a fruitless search I grab one of each, size Extra Husky, and put them on. When I walk out drowning in this sea of vestments, looking like I've shrunk, the priest takes a gander, shakes his head, and says, "Saints preserve us!" with an annoyed tone. Meanwhile, an oldie-but-goodie Catholic joke that always breaks me up pops into my head, so naturally I share it with the other altar boy just before Mass starts. (What's black and white, black and white, black and white? A nun rolling down a hill.)

We walk in procession down the aisle behind the priest, both of us carrying a small candle, each of which is shaking because we're snickering from the joke. I realize our behavior could get us a ticket to eternal damnation, so I straighten up to hold my candle high and proceed to singe a large patch of hair on the back of the good Father's head. This produces a brief puff of smoke that smells like dandruff shampoo, and a groan from the victim, who just spent three dollars on a haircut.

Later, we both get his standard lecture for altar boys about goofing off on the job that includes, "And don't think for one minute I don't know about the wine!"

These days, I treat my Catholicism with the proper reverence, thanks to a deeper understanding and respect. Shamefully, though, sometimes I still snicker in church. Lord help me, but that nun joke is funny.

Zagging When I Should Have Zigged

BACK IN KINDERGARTEN I WAS UTTERLY HUMILIATED by a pair of scissors. I know this sounds overly-dramatic – which my long-suffering wife will tell you is one of my major character flaws, right behind dozens of others – but it's true.

My classmates and I were handed an extra-long sheet of paper with a cartoonish train mimeographed onto it. Our assignment was to color it, then cut it out. It was kind of thrilling, because my mother wouldn't let me have scissors at home. "You'll cut off somebody's hand and then they'll come crying to me," was her reasoning.

Now, the whole idea of lopping off somebody's hands with scissors, then trying to glue them back on, intrigued my five-year-old brain. My little sister never used her hands for much other than flushing valuable heirlooms down the toilet, so she was a prime candidate. With her tiny hands it wouldn't take much glue, and if we were out of glue she could eat with her feet until my mom bought more at the store.

But to my parents' credit, by the time I came along they had learned to keep dangerous things out of their children's reach. Sure, my older brothers and sisters are now walking around with the odd appendage missing because my dad let them play with scissors before my mother made him wise up. They still complain about it, but my mother reminds them that when they were young she and Dad were still inexperienced, and kids don't come with an instruction manual, and if they would for Pete's sake stop whining about it and wear big hats nobody would even notice their missing ears.

So I felt delightfully wicked when my kindergarten teacher handed me a pair of blunt kiddie scissors. The metal gleamed, and they felt cold in my hand. I practiced opening and closing them, imagining they were a shark's mouth that could chew all the hair off Alvie Dinkle, who always took too many graham crackers during snack time and made fun of the tap-dancing gingerbread men covering my nap mat.

My teacher, who unfairly profiled me from the day I lost my pants during a fire drill, looked uneasy. She was still getting over a previous disaster involving me and the economy-sized bottle of hand lotion on her desk, which – let's face it – could have happened to anyone who was fooling around with it after being told not to. She kept looking from the scissors I was gripping to my bulging eyes and back again, probably wondering if anyone would notice if she locked me in the utility closet the rest of the school year.

"You just be careful," she pleaded more than advised. "Because when you accidently give yourself a lobotomy I don't want your parents crying to me."

I asked what a lobotomy is, and she mumbled something like, "Don't tempt me." Then she went to the bottom drawer in her desk, where she kept the same kind of stomach medicine my dad took whenever he'd Had It Up To Here With You Kids.

Well, I got busy cutting out my train, which, after my unimaginative coloring job, looked like it had derailed into a bowl of pea soup. The problem was that I am a lefty born into a right-handed world, so the standard blunt kiddie scissors wouldn't cooperate. The more I tried a left-handed zig around the sharp corners of the cartoon boxcars the more the right-handed scissors would zag and slice off a wheel or the head of someone on board.

Even at my tender age I could see what was coming. My teachers would hang the trains around the room and invite the parents to come and see the fine job their children did. And every time someone reached the far corner of the room where mine was displayed there would be muffled gasps, then quiet whispers among the moms and dads: "Well, you know I heard he's just not right."

I looked up at the teacher, who sat glumly at her desk, swigging from the medicine bottle like it was Happy Hour. When she saw my mangled train she took a last full-throated chug, belched, and announced she was going somewhere to lie down, preferably miles away.

Everything turned out fine. My teacher got her transfer, and my mother has the paper train tucked safely away in an old cardboard box, where no one can judge it. With her tutoring I did eventually master scissors.

She's always saying how I owe her big time for sacrificing so much to teach me, but I tell her to stop bellyaching and keep wearing a big hat so no one will notice.

Second Grade, Valentine's Day

EACH OF US BRINGS OUR STORE-BOUGHT, SIGNED valentines to school. Mine are heart-shaped, with sentiments like "Be Mine" and "Forever Yours." There's a blond girl with pigtails named Susan who sits two rows over from me that I "like." I'm not really sure all of what that entails. I heard one of my older sisters tell her friend that she "liked" a boy in her class named Eugene, so I wanted to "like" a girl in mine. So I told everybody I knew that I "liked" Susan.

In art class the day before, our teacher, Sister Mary Mumbler (at least that's what everybody calls her – the woman can't speak up to save her life) showed us how to make and decorate construction paper pouches to hold the valentines we would receive from admiring classmates. Now The Mumbler instructs us to pass our pouches around.

Well, I'm not about to give my valentines to just anybody. Norman Fenway, the creep who forced me to sit in mucilage he squirted on my chair, certainly doesn't deserve one. Neither does Veronica Penswacki, who everyone – even The Mumbler – knows is totally stuck-up just because her dad owns a corner store and she gets all the free penny candy she wants.

No, I want my valentines to go to nice kids, like Tommy Guthright, who taught me how to hit any urinal in the boys' lavatory from two feet away, and Jeanine Howk, who let me borrow her red Crayola one day during Science when I was drawing a diseased amoeba. But mostly, I want my valentines to go to Susan.

When classmates' pouches come across my desk, except for Tommy's and Jeanine's I only pretend to put valentines in them. Then I get Susan's. It's colored red and pink, and she drew hearts on it with arrows through them and a picture of a blond girl with pigtails blowing kisses, which are drawn as big red puckered lips floating through the air.

I notice that inside, right at the top, is a huge heart-shaped valentine from Matthew Gold, Mr. Second Grade Dreamboat with the nice corduroy pants and patent leather buckle shoes. It has a cartoon on it of two puppies with lovey-dovey hearts circling their heads, and one puppy saying to the other, "I'd be doggone happy if you were my Valentine!" In his gold star-winning penmanship Matthew added, "I like you more than David Coehrs does XXX."

My seven-year-old heart plummets to my wool socks. Anyone can tell you it's no fair for Matthew to "like" Susan when I already have dibs on "liking" her. And Matthew Gold of all people, who has nice thick hair and an A in Arithmetic, and one of those coveted Jonny Quest lunchboxes with the matching Thermos. I am crushed, because I wear my brother's hand-me-downs, go home for lunch and the buckle on one of my scuffed shoes is crooked.

So, I take the rest of my valentines, which include one I am supposed to give to The Mumbler and one I accidentally signed for myself, and stuff them into Susan's pouch, which pooches out and makes her look extra popular. But in the end it doesn't matter, because she tells on me and then pins Matthew's valentine to the front of her dress. Tommy, who sits by them in the cafeteria, tells me later they held hands under the table and shared a raisin cookie.

After being forced to retrieve all but one of my valentines from Susan – who now smirks at me like Valerie Penswacki always does – and distribute them among all my classmates, I decide to "like" Jeanine instead. To show my true feelings for her, I'm going to give her my picture of the diseased amoeba, which I got a B+ on.

I Couldn't Get a Date in a Brothel

PROM TIME IS APPROACHING, AND OUR MIDDLE son is going. He's already bought tickets for himself and his girlfriend, and on a recent weekend we rented him a tuxedo. Seeing as how this kid never – and I mean never – wears anything but nylon wind pants and T-shirts, talking him into a tux for the occasion was tantamount to talking a Hare Krishna into combat fatigues. He raised a humongous stink, so we had to bribe him – and when that didn't work, sedate him – to get him fitted for the proper outfit.

I told my brown-eyed girl if he continues to balk about it we'll take the tickets and go instead. I don't mind being dressed in a monkey suit for a few hours if it means getting away with her to someplace romantic. We'd probably have to dance to the same God-awful music the boys play at home, which turned my goatee gray overnight, but I can stand it if she can.

I wasn't fortunate enough to go to my own prom, because (a) the only female willing to go with me was my mother, and my only back-up was my grandmother, whose fruity old-lady perfume always preceded her by about an hour. It was suggested I take my sister, but (b) I didn't have nearly the money she demanded, and (c) I liked to think I had my pride, even though the truth was, I didn't.

I even had a secret prom date picked out – Laurie Hermoine – a junior with a cute face and huge brown eyes. In my perpetual state of extremely sheltered Catholic naivete I didn't realize she was considered a wild bad girl who dabbled in "stuff," as my classmate Wiffy put it. Wiffy made no secret of the fact that occasionally he also dabbled in "stuff," so he knew who the "stuffers" were. Like any geek who spent the bulk of his Saturday nights alone eating frozen pizza and listening to Casey Kasem's top 40, I was stunned by this revelation. I had it bad for Laurie, worshipping from afar and imagining us and our thirty-two children.

So I spent that evening at a pitiful event called the Unprom, which was coordinated by others like me who couldn't have gotten a date in a brothel. We held it in a local park, armed with hamburger patties, potato salad, Frisbees and broken hearts, and tried very hard to have a good time. That was tough, given the fact our cooler classmates were in the school gymnasium enjoying "Moonlight and Heaven," complete with tinfoil stars, a fake waterfall and little take-home centerpieces filled with M&Ms.

I sat beside the park's pond as the sun faded, nursing a cola and sulking over the fact that Laurie was probably at the prom with a fellow "stuffer." I imagined him driving her there in a smokin' Corvette with louvers on the rear windshield and an eight-track player blasting out *Hotel California*. I imagined him holding her a little too closely at the dance, and giving her a hickey as they swayed to the band's rendition of *Tonight's The Night*.

It was pure torture, and I chugged the cola straight down to forget my misery. In my company, she would have been transported in my dad's boxy Plymouth and endured my sweaty palms and armpit stains. But I would have been a perfect gentlemen, which, in retrospect, I'm sure she wasn't looking for.

Then my friend Tom walked over to the pond with two slices of watermelon and commiserated. I told him about Laurie, and he said, "You know she's into stuff," and I replied, "Yeah, Wiffy told me" and morosely spit watermelon seeds. Then we played half-hearted Frisbee

Here's hoping my boy has the time of his life. And, Laurie, if you're out there, I still think it was your loss.

Just Write it Down!

PAUSING, I GO OVER THE LIST IN MY HEAD AGAIN. I know I'm missing something vital, but can't for the life of me remember what. It started with C, or maybe V, and it's important.

She told me to write it all down, the same way she does every time she sends me on an errand for three or more items. She'll hand me paper and pen and tell me to lose my Superman complex because, despite all the bragging about my superior total recall, I will forget every one of the items by the time I reach our car in the driveway. She'll say to stop trying to impress her with my supposed razor-sharp memory and just write it all down, before I make her ulcer flare again.

But I'm a guy, and it's our job during such marital stand-offs to act stubborn and usually more than a little dumb. So before this trip to the store I tried to prove my brain power by reciting all the U.S. presidents in chronological order. And I was golden until I reach Lincoln, at which point I struggled, thinking the next president's name began with K, or possibly Z. She rolled her eyes and said to stop humiliating myself, and I cursed myself for paying more attention in American History class to Sandy Fleener's cute legs than to the lessons.

I always do this, she tells me with a groan. I swear I'll

remember everything in my crystal-clear memory without benefit of a written list. She'll reel off the items, and before her mouth is closed I'm tapping my temple, saying, "Got it" with a cocky grin. Then I'll come back an hour later with a dozen heads of Korean cabbage and a naked-lady keychain and swear that's what she asked for.

So now I'm standing in the store, thinking really hard until I get a spiky pain behind my right eye, and something tells me the item I can't remember could begin with T. So I cruise the store aisles, looking at everything beginning with T, but nothing rings my bell. I'm positive she doesn't want a tiki torch or a ten-pack of salmon fritters, and I'm almost nine-tenths sure she isn't wanting topical cream for a spore infection.

I can already imagine the aggravated look on her face when I return home without something she asked for. It's a look that bores right through your skull and out the back of your head, where it will actually shatter any object directly behind you. I've warned her about it, but occasionally she'll forget and shoot it at me, and then we'll have to replace whatever household item I'm standing directly in front of. One time when she zinged me "the look" it struck and perfectly cooked a chicken she had been thawing for dinner on the counter behind me.

"Why can't you ever just write things down?" she'll plead as she pops three more antacids.

Because she doesn't understand the pride I have in my gift of recollection. Heck, I can still remember the names of kindergarten classmates. Well, maybe one – that Joe or Pete Somebody with the crooked tooth who liked to pull my hair during sing-a-longs. And there was Bernard or Brian

Something, that rheumy kid who chewed with his mouth open during snack time.

I'll gradually remember the forgotten item, although I may have to step it up. I've been in this store for so long they're closing up and shutting off the lights. The store manager is pointing to his watch, yelling, "Tick tock, buddy! We'd like to go home!"

Yeah, me too, if I could remember which street I live on.

Used Cat Litter and Chocolate Frosting

SO ANYWAY, BY THE TIME WE REACH THE STORE it has closed. "I'm going to flunk this project!" the 15-year-old wails, looking at me accusingly. "It's all your fault! You didn't speed like I told you!"

If you recall, his school science project was due a week ago. The only reason my brown-eyed girl and I knew about it at all was because his teacher informed us in a terse e-mail. He explained that the only two students who hadn't turned in the project were our son and a foreign exchange student who is still learning English. After lots of groveling on our part the teacher agreed to give twenty four more hours.

"You had almost a month to do this project," my wife scolds our son.

"I forgot about it!" the boy says defensively. "People forget things, you know!"

"Especially when they're caught playing video games when they're supposed to be doing homework," his mother replies.

We've been through this little game with him before. As I prepared to drive him to school one morning he informed us that, by the way, he was supposed to turn in a clay map of our state that morning, complete with accurate representations of its topography and accompanied by a ten-page report on its history and major industries. He didn't do it, he told us, because by the time he remembered to bring home the packet of clay he was assigned it had dried up in his locker. And then – honest, he insisted – he tried to make homemade clay from a tub of ready-made chocolate frosting he found in a kitchen cupboard, but then it didn't mix well with gravel he stole from the fish bowl, so he ate the rest instead. And if he didn't do the map, well, what use was writing the report?

We could tell he had worked hard on this excuse, probably using as much time to devise it as he would have used completing the project. He spun it with a lot of hokey earnest and pathos, pausing occasionally to squeeze out a tear and place his hand over his heart in an expression of regret.

"Uh-huh," is all we could manage to say as we bit our tongues almost in half to restrain ourselves from screaming bloody murder. When he got home that afternoon he found every electronic device he owned confiscated, along with his CD and DVD collections and his privilege to see the outside world for awhile. But we were civil about it: We both squeezed out a tear and placed our hands over our hearts in an expression of regret.

So now my car sits idling in the empty parking lot of a store fifteen miles from home that carries the specific supplies we need for his overdue science project. The store isn't open, even though our child was absolutely positive before I drove him there that he knew the correct store hours – ABSOLUTELY POSITIVE. We find out later that "absolutely positive" meant his friend told him, which, if you know the friend – who never wears a shirt, so I guess we can be grateful he does wear pants – you can understand why we're at the store after closing.

"I told you to speed!" the 15-year-old repeats. "We would've gotten here on time if you sped!"

"Why did I need to speed if you were absolutely positive what hours they're open?" I ask.

"Because!" he sputters, grasping for any straws he can find. "Because – you know – just in case! And now you've ruined my grade!"

When we get back home, he does the best he can on the project with what household materials he finds. He discovered ready-made chocolate frosting works better with used cat litter, but a school project has probably never been so sticky – whew – or smelly.

Women – The Final Frontier

JUST WHEN YOU THINK YOU KNOW EVERYTHING, you don't. After living this long with my wife I thought I knew absolutely everything there is to know about dealing with women. In my younger days, I never would have had the ignorance or the confidence to make such an arrogant statement, but you learn from experience. And I learned that I don't know squat.

The way I reached this epiphany was, I asked her, "Are you out of your mind?" as she was about to absentmindedly place a plastic bowl in our heated oven. She's had brain overload lately, what with studying non-stop for her nursing certificate, working the night shift full-time, the boys tipping over our car in the driveway and swearing it was accidental, and the cats suddenly becoming incontinent everywhere after feasting on homemade cat food I was experimenting with.

So in the frazzled, gnarly condition she was in, questioning her sanity was, to say the least, not so bright.

"Am I out of my mind?" she barked back. "That's what you have the nerve to ask me? With everything I have on my plate? While you stand there stuffing a cupcake in your mouth with apparently nothing better to do than insult me?"

"Uh ..." I answered, because saying anything else would only have gotten me deeper into the dog house.

"You know how insane my schedule is. You know I'm exhausted and not exactly thinking straight. Do you think maybe, 'Do you need help?' might have been a more sensitive thing to ask?"

"Uh ..." I said again, trying for dear life to hang onto my sinking ship.

"You really should start thinking before you open your mouth, because when you don't you make it obvious your brain is marinated in 'jerk.'" (She later apologized for that parting zinger – which anyone will tell you was a bullseye – because she has class and decency. Apparently, those are ingredients God forgot to include when He made me.)

So I tried to make up through our locked bedroom door. "I didn't mean it that way," I called. "I should have been nicer. I've just never seen you do something that dumb before."

The boys were watching this drama play out, and even they were aghast.

"Aw, dude, that is so wrong," the 15-year-old said, wincing and shaking his head. "Don't you know anything about girls?" He once had a girlfriend for three whole hours, and he was showing more sense than me.

"I mean ... I didn't mean you're dumb, exactly," I stammered through the door. "I just mean ... well ... you have to admit that putting a plastic bowl in a hot oven is ... is ... "

While I was trying to formulate a polite description that wouldn't send me from the dog house into the dungeon the bedroom floor flew open.

"Is what?" she asked, eyes flashing. "Is stupid? Is idiotic? Is criminally moronic?"

"I would never call you criminally moronic!" I said patronizingly. "Even though you almost put a plastic bowl in a hot oven, I still consider you basically smart."

"BASICALLY smart?"

The boys actually flinched. "Aw, dude! Crash and burn!"

I don't know why I kept talking. None of what I'd already said had left my mouth in the same way it had formed in my mind, and I was hanging by my fingertips.

"Oh, you betcha!" I told her. "You're a real keeper. I've always told my mom that. Just ask her, although you might want to ask before I tell her about the bowl."

It's been three days, and I finally managed to repair the bedroom door from her final slam. My wife forgave me after I promised never to talk again, and it's not so bad.

It gives me a chance to perfect my indignant eye-rolling.

Teen-speak: So I was Like ... Dude!

"SO HE'S LIKE, 'WHAT'S YOUR DEAL?' AND I'M LIKE, 'What's your deal?'And he's, like, looking at me, so I start walking away. But then he's like, 'Dude!' So I was like, 'Aw, Dude!' and he was like, 'Uh-uh, Dude!' and now it's, like, so not sick."

The 15-year-old is telling me about something "epic" that happened at school. His blow-by-blow account has lasted ten minutes and I still have no clue what he's talking about.

"So then when I saw Pocky I was like, 'Du-u-ude!' and he was like, 'Yeah, dude, I heard. That's not even sick.' And I was like, 'Dude, seriously!' And he was like, 'Not even sick, Dude.'"

I think I might have the gist of this epic event. I think somebody's mad at somebody, and I think somebody else thinks it's not sick. And I think this sick slang doesn't really mean sick, but the opposite of sick, which is – well?

"So Pocky goes and tells him, like, 'Dude, this in not even sick.' And he's like, to Pocky, 'Dude, don't even.' And Pocky's like, 'Chillax,' and the dude is like, 'You chillax, bro.' And I'm just, like, bumming."

Okay, chillax is maybe a little trickier to decipher, but I'm going to see this through because it's the most genuinely lucid conversation I've had with this kid in ages. Usually, he speaks with such a pronounced mumble it's like talking to a Ubangi tribesman.

"So, like, what happened next?" I ask.

"You kiddin', Dude? It was, like, epic! Pocky's like, 'You are so not sick.' And the dude's like, 'Sicker than you, Dude.' And Pocky's like, 'No way, Dude!' Then the dude's like, 'Mortal Kombat, Dude - tonight!' And Pocky's like, 'Tonight, Dude!'"

"Wait, wait," I interrupt. "What's Mortal Kombat?"

"Du-u-ude!" the 15-year-old says, mortified. "What's Mortal Kombat? SERIOUSLY?"

I'm losing him. Apparently, ignorance of Mortal Kombat is criminal, tantamount to liking meatloaf and boy bands.

"Oh - Mortal Kombat! I thought you said Mortal Wombat!" I say lamely to save myself.

"Mortal what?"

"Wombat. It's a quadrupedal marsupial indigenous to Australia."

"Quadra-what?"

"Not important. So anyway, you said Pocky was like, 'Tonight, Dude?'"

"Yeah! So they're, like, gonna face off tonight! It's gonna be, like, epic!"

"Wow, that does sound epic," I try to say with awe. Yes, I'm patronizing him. But our longest previous conversation on record went something like this: Me – "What's up?" Him – "(Ubangi mumble)." So I'm hanging onto this one for dear life.

"Yeah, Dude, epic!" he says. "Pocky's gonna destroy him!"

I doubt it. Pocky can't even spell destroy. Pocky can't

even spell Pocky.

"So we're all, like, meeting at his house at midnight to watch!"

"Whoa!" I say. "Midnight?"

"Yeah! It's so epic!"

"No. It's a school night."

He gives me his best "You're So Not Sick" look. He must practice it in the mirror.

"Pocky said you'd, like, say that. He was like, 'Dude, he's gonna say it's a school night. He's gonna be so not sick about letting you go.'"

Know this about Pocky: If he were my child he'd be getting regular brain scans.

"You're not going anywhere on a school night, and especially not at midnight."

"Dude, you're, like, so not sick."

"And Dude, you're, like, so not going."

He's angry now, and so not talking to me. He's, like, deliberately playing that totally noisy video game I can't stand. Pocky would probably tell him to, like, keep playing it loudly until I give in. Pocky's so not sick. And he can't spell "loudly" either.

I am the great Rochowtski!

WATCHING RANDY ROCHOWTSKI TAKE A header off his garage roof was a thing of beauty. Kids used to come from blocks around to see it. Being one of Randy's friends, I always got a choice seat on his lawn to witness this death-defying feat. Once everyone got settled, Randy would stand on the edge of the roof wearing the blue blanket from his bed like a cape and his genuine Lone Ranger mask over his eyes. He'd take a long rip from a bottle of Hires root beer, belch with satisfaction, then hurtle over the edge, yelling "Cowabunga!"

He had an old mattress lying on the concrete below him, but it wasn't thick enough to prevent a somewhat sickening thud when he hit it headfirst. Each time his audience would gasp and jump to its feet, certain Randy's skull would split down the middle, and invariably one of the more skittish girls or boys would sick up in Randy's mother's hydrangea shrub. But he always leapt up after landing, shaking his head the way Wile E. Coyote does in the cartoons after getting beaned with an anvil, and proclaim, "I am the great Rochowtski!" Although sometimes after bashing himself like that he would forget his name and simply say, "I am the great!"

On weekends he would do four shows a day, including a matinee, and one time after school he offered to dive without the mattress if we'd all chip in a quarter for his trouble. That was the day his mother finally pulled herself away from her soaps long enough to realize what had been going on, and screamed, "RANDALL STEVEN ROCHOWTSKI, ARE YOU OUT OF YOUR MIND?"

Well, we kids scattered to the winds, and Randy was miffed because he was going to use the quarters to buy the economy bag of gumballs he'd been eyeing at the corner store. His mother, who smoked unfiltered Lucky Strikes and always had brown fingertips, checked him for a concussion. When she determined he didn't have one she smacked him a good one across the head and made him sit on the back porch steps while she went in to finish *Search For Tomorrow*. And that ended both Randy's regular and matinee performances.

I mention all this because I'm still amazed that as kids we managed to get away with doing things like that without killing ourselves. Granted, Randy would occasionally slip into a daze and drool for five minutes, but he grew up to be a wealthy, respected lawyer. So what if he's known to involuntarily blurt out "I am the great Rochowtski!" during courtroom proceedings. He owns a mansion and a Jaguar.

My mother always said children have especially tough guardian angels; otherwise, like Randy, they'd always be knocking their brains out. She believed her own children were evidence of this added protection, as we constantly walked away from daredevil escapades with our roller skates, bicycles and the higher branches of our 80-foot tall backyard tree needing a Band-Aid rather than a body cast or a wheelchair.

Considering all the stunts my own kids pulled while growing up, I also believe it's divine intervention. Nothing else explains why they're not walking around limbless and with only about sixteen good brains cells between them. Following all the near-misses of theirs I walked in on, and had been just seconds too late to prevent, it's a wonder my hair isn't completely gray and my stomach full of bleeding ulcers.

What I really could have used each time was Mrs. Rochowtski's hydrangea shrub. I mean before all those barfy kids ruined it.

A Fella Can Dream

THIS TIME EVERY YEAR THE PRIVATE HIGH school I attended sends out a glossy, dozen-page reminder to alumni that it's still there and could use a few of their hard-earned bucks. It also likes to rub my face in the fact that all my former classmates are considerably better off than me.

If my brown-eyed girl sees it first among the mail she snatches it and tries to hide it from me. She especially doesn't want me to peruse the "Class Updates" section, because it only depresses me and makes me wonder where I went wrong. She knows if I flip through it she'll have to endure a long month of my moping around, shaking my head, saying things like, "Paulie Kunkle is a real estate magnate. In sophomore geography class Paulie Kunkle thought Tokyo was the capitol of New Hampshire, and now he's making three million a year."

Back then everybody thought Paulie was dumber than mud, just like Weird Wendy Mooney, who ate a big black ant on a fifty-cent dare, and liked it so much dipped in ketchup she starting bringing them in her lunch. Weird Wendy now markets a wildly successful line of Goth clothing, and can afford to spend a couple months each year in Europe, although she probably never travels beyond Transylvania.

I'll bet she has one of those honking huge 99-inch plasma flatscreen televisions in the equally huge den of her fifty-room mansion, the same kind of television I can't afford and drool over in the electronics section of the local big box store. Her mansion probably also has an indoor Olympic-sized pool similar to the imaginary one a fellow classmate once convinced her was in our school. She kept searching for it after buying open-swim passes from him.

Not that I did badly in high school. But I wasn't a rocket scientist like Elaine Aubrey, who in our junior year underwent surgery to have her IQ lowered a few hundred points to prevent her head from exploding. I struggled through math, and caused multiple evacuations of the chemistry lab, and wrote articles and a column for the school newspaper that would make anyone who read them wonder why I didn't spend even more time with the school psychologist. I wasn't in the top ten of my senior class, and I wasn't inducted into the National Honor Society. But I did write a one-act play in Basic Comp that my teacher, Sister Mary Denouement, reviewed as "demented trash, yet oddly compelling."

So now I write for a living, and live in a modest house with a wife and 2.5 kids and 5.4 cats. We buy mostly generic brands at the grocery store, not to mention the least expensive motor oil, which makes the old heap sputter and spew noxious fumes blamed for burning off the nose hair of those standing nearby. We don't vacation in San Trope, or wear Yves Saint Laurent, and we only buy that really premium ice cream we like when it's on sale.

Then I read in the class updates that Mike Perski, who was best known for armpit noises and sneaking into the girls locker room, "is a neurosurgeon who was recently awarded the prestigious Triple Golden Scalpel for his revolutionary work in brain transplants and painless hemorrhoid extractions. Dr. Perski currently resides in the exclusive Brentwood section of Los Angeles with his trophy wife, Bootsy, and his prized Lamborghini."

Maybe I'm just a late bloomer. Maybe that critically-acclaimed novel I've been intending to write, the one that will make tons of money and Hollywood will option, is right around the corner.

I can see my class update now: "David J. Coehrs is a novelist whose latest work, described as 'demented trash, yet oddly compelling,' is set to become a feature film. He and his wife recently purchased that really premium ice cream they like, and it wasn't even on sale."

A fella can dream.

Getting Old Sucks

BOY, AM I DUMB. I MEAN, I'VE DONE SOME DUMB things in my life, but this one easily fits in my personal Dumb Hall of Fame. That is, if there's any room for it. Since cataract surgery earlier this year, my eyesight has transitioned from near-sightedness to far-sightedness. That means whereas the print from books, magazines, the Internet and the taboo material I keep hidden under my mattress used to fairly leap out at my vision, now it cringes back and forces me to chase after it.

That requires the help of reading glasses, although I never thought I'd be one of those old people who would have them. But I remember my Grandpa Eddie holding reading material at arm's length while he squinted this way and that and mumbled as he tried to decipher it. I was six years old, and Grandpa Eddie's constantly moving, squinty face made him look like he was morphing into a bulldog, which, when you're six, can scare you right into a bathroom accident, and don't ask how I know this. So I decided right then to get reading glasses if I ever needed them.

But after the surgery, when I would look at the front page of the newspaper and see nothing but fuzz because my eyesight had transitioned, I was determined not to allow my optometrist, who for some inexplicable reason thinks my name is Buzzy, to prescribe an expensive pair of reading lenses.

Instead, I ran to the health care department of the local big box and bought a cheap pair of those ready-made old-people reading glasses. They are displayed on a huge kiosk that is brightly colored so old, far-sighted people don't plow right into it when they're two feet away. The lenses are made of varying degrees of magnified plastic that, when you wear them, make letters of the alphabet the size of low-flying planes.

So I took home a pair of the most flattering old-people style I could find and looked at the newspaper again, and this time every letter on it looked as big as the E on top of an eye chart. The problem was, I needed to take the glasses with me everywhere in case I needed to read something important, like someone's will if they got squashed by a bus and left me something.

Well, I didn't want to look like an old fuddy carrying around ready-made old-people reading glasses, so I began hooking one of the stems inside my shirt at the collar. I checked myself in mirrors a couple thousand times to make sure that glasses lying flat across my chest looked rad, and in fact they did. But one day they suddenly went missing. I was positive I had them hooked tightly over my shirt when I left home, and here they were gone. After a cursory, then more involved search for them at home and in and around the front car seat, and after back-tracking to every place I had visited, I gave up the search. It was weird how they had vanished without a trace.

I went back to the kiosk, this time banging into it despite the bright colors, and picked up a similar pair of the ready-made glasses. Within a day they also disappeared, seemingly into a black hole, and despite all the swearing I did they didn't come back.

So yesterday I purchased a third pair, practically gluing them to my shirt. When I parked in the lot at work I pulled off my seat belt – and for the first time noticed it hook onto my glasses as it slid back in place and fling them over my shoulder.

I now have three pairs of cheap, ready-made old-people glasses – the pair I just bought and the two previous pairs, all of which I found lying on the floor of the car behind the driver's seat.

Stop laughing.

Anything Night

SO ANYWAY, THE LINE IS GETTING LONGER, THE customers more impatient, and the pizza slice more elusive by the moment.

Believe me, I'm trying to follow protocol. I have the little spatula in hand, trying to do the right thing, but the food just won't cooperate. Only me, I think grimly as I chase it around the buffet table. I can't imagine this happening to anybody but me.

We're at a pizza place for dinner because it was either that or "Anything Night" at home. Anything Night occurs when the very last thing my brown-eyed girl and I feel like doing is cooking. We look at each other, and we're both exhausted from dealing with work and teenaged boys who, on a good day, can drive you eight kinds of crazy and lead you to chug antacid by the gallon. So the thought of pulling out the pots and pans and trying to make a pound of hamburger seem enticing makes us cringe. I say, "What do you want to do about dinner?" knowing full well that neither of us plans to make it. Then she says, "I don't know. What do you want to do?" in a tone that suggests it's going to be Anything Night and it's every man for himself.

Of course, the boys are thrilled with Anything Night, because it gives them the opportunity to eat stuff for dinner we wouldn't normally let them get away with. The 15-year-old pulls out a box of cereal with absolutely no nutritional value and enough sugar to shoot him to Venus, and follows that up with half a dozen cupcakes and a sleeve of cookies. His brother chooses instant cup-o-soup made entirely of preservatives. "Eat something healthy!" we order, and they both smirk because, well, they're boys, and unless we intervened regularly there wouldn't be a single vitamin or mineral present in their entire bodies.

Anyway, we hit this particular pizza buffet, where the boys immediately grab plates and attack like starving badgers, loading up as if we keep them tied in a closet and feed them only scraps every other week. I politely peruse the pizza choices, and demurely go after a mushroom and black olive combination. I corral a slice on one of the little spatulas provided, and that's when the cheese hits the fan.

The slice slides off the spatula and lands on the serving table. "Whoops!" I say comically to the person standing next to me, indicating that I'm not always such a klutz, even though anyone who knows me knows better. I try to scoop the pizza slice back onto the spatula, but it's having none of that, and decides instead to land back on the serving table, this time upside down. The person next to me arches an eyebrow, and I giggle nervously and go after the slice again. And again and again.

By now I'm holding up the buffet line, and a little boy whines "I'm HUNGRY!" and bonks me with his plate. I have chased what's left of the combination mushroom and black olive slice around the table several times. But now it's become more than a slippery pizza slice. It's a vendetta, and I'm determined to win.

The boys sit at our table, their cheeks stuffed with pepperoni, and they start a low chant of "Go, go, go!" until their mother pokes them and says to knock it off. She looks at me with pleading eyes that beg me to stop embarrassing myself, but I'm too determined to win. I'm going to chase this stupid pizza slice from here to Timbuktu if necessary, and it's going to land on my plate.

After several more laps, and some pithy threats from the restaurant manager, I finally scoop the mangled slice onto the spatula. "Hah!" I yell triumphantly, and lift the spatula high while I do a very unnecessary victory dance. I then slap the pizza onto my plate, where it promptly slides off and hits the floor.

Just one more lap around the restaurant should do it.

Teenagers, Logic and Oxymorons

There's a door lying in our carport. No kidding, an actual wooden door in a wooden frame. It's lying flat, so that if you open it and try to walk through you'll get a face full of concrete. Don't ask me how I know this, just accept it.

The boys carried the door home from someone's front lawn. The previous owner obviously saw the sense in tossing it out, but my kids did not. On their way home from school they saw this complete door just sitting there, and their imaginations obviously ran wild. Apparently, the possibilities for it seemed endless, because they hoisted it on their shoulders and paraded it to our house.

When I heard the ruckus I looked out the front window, then commented, "The boys brought a door home," just as casually as if I was saying, "Shaun across the street is running naked around his yard with a waffle iron again." My brown-eyed girl peeked out the window at the spectacle and replied, "Oh," as if every day the boys brought home something just as unusual, like an ostrich with a mullet.

When they came through the front door I waited for them to explain the extra door, which they didn't, instead heading straight for the refrigerator. So I let them have their afterschool snack, then watched as they jumped on the computer like always, and still nothing was said about the door.

"Um ... you guys brought home a door," I said to stimulate conversation. Neither offered a response. "I noticed it even has a frame attached," I continued. Still nothing. "So ... I just checked, and we have plenty of doors."

"It's for our video," they said together without looking up.

"What video?" I asked. I know I shouldn't have, but I've been in kind of a rut lately and thought this conversation might just add some excitement.

"We decided to do a video, and we're going to use the door," the middle one said.

"A video about what?"

The 14-year-old rolled his eyes. "We don't know yet, but the door is our prop."

This is why I'm glad I'm no longer a teenager. I never understood my own mind when I was their age, so I sure as heck don't understand theirs.

"And when are you going to shoot this video?"

The middle one rolled his eyes. "We don't know. But now we have a door for it."

I know there's probably logic there somewhere. I just don't have the kind of time it would take to sift through their teenaged brains to find it.

"So until then it's going to lie in the carport," I concluded. They looked at each other as though I had just sucked out my own brain through a straw in my nose. "Well – duh!"

"And where do you suggest I put the car?"

They shrugged in tandem.

"Can you see why bringing an entire door home without a real plan might have been a little – I don't know – impulsive?"

The middle one got exasperated. "So now you're saying we can't do the video?"

"Heaven forbid," I said tiredly, my fingers trying to pinch back the headache. "After all, you already have the door."

Of course, this was all weeks ago. Since then the door has been rained on, tripped over, exposed to frost and generally ignored. If they bring home a window next, I'm going to use both to build a little cabin where I can hide until they move away.

Three Stepsons and a Newborn?

JOKE IF YOU WILL, BUT I TOLD MY BROWN-EYED girl that if she ever gave birth to our child I would stay with her in the delivery room, even if it meant fainting or worse. And, boy howdy, would it ever.

Of course, it's a moot point. Having one teenage and two adult stepsons, no natural children of my own and a biological clock with a busted spring, I can guarantee that joyous event will never happen. Besides, my wife and I are at an age where, instead of bringing home an addition, we're doing everything possible to encourage the kids we have to leave. We have been locking up everything of interest to them, including the bathrooms, and swearing we don't know where the keys are. We have also painstakingly altered a copy of the U.S. Constitution as proof that we are not obligated to feed them anymore, and can, in fact, legally eat them if we run out of food.

The 15-year-old, who is usually in the process of stuffing anything he finds edible into his mouth, likes to tease us that he is never leaving. He likes to inhale an entire loaf of bread and a whole jar of peanut butter, smack his lips and announce his plans to snack like that the rest of his life. I know he's just trying to yank my chain, but believe me, watching the way he can suck down entire cows and pigs when he's hungry would chill anyone to the bone. If he stays with us interminably I can only imagine the carnage.

But I digress. I simply want to reassure my wife I'm a faithful and devoted husband who will walk through fire for her so long as nothing gets singed. I want her to know that, despite my deplorable history of utter squeamishness, I would insist on witnessing the arrival of our hypothetical baby, even if it meant ralfing and pitching head first into the doctor's lap.

I read once that Prince Philip, the Duke of Edinburgh, was playing polo at the time Queen Elizabeth gave birth to one of their children. I was appalled that he considered a few chukkers more important than watching his child emerge into the world all purple and squishy and looking like it's not done cooking. "Egad!" I could imagine him saying frightfully upon his first look. "What in heaven's name is that? Put it back, and bring me another!"

No, I would never be that insensitive. My wife has already related to me how when a child is born it can look more like a salamander than a human being. She said it takes a few minutes of cleaning, shaping and molding for a baby to look adorable and like something you'd actually want to take home. She said sometimes its head can be shaped like it was stretched through a taffy press, and you have to wait for the "boing!" when it snaps back to regulation size.

I myself was not an attractive baby, looking more like a wrinkly old man wearing a diaper. My brown-eyed girl will look at my professionally-produced baby picture and say with a forced smile, "You were so cute!" and if I had the IQ of a meatball I'd probably believe her. Yet I'll accept her blatant but well-meaning lie, and say something like, "You really think so?" to which she'll always reply, "Sure, sure, cute" and then change the subject.

Which is another reason why having a child together is a moot point. Setting aside the fact we're both a bit long in the tooth for a newborn, I simply can't imagine the kid inheriting my taffy head, which I've waited for years to "boing!" back to regulation size. I'd wear a hat to hide it but that's like trying to cover a corn dog with a Dixie cup.

Ghosts of Cheese Fries Past

So I'm sitting at home Friday night, watching a cheesy, low-rent horror flick on the tube – the vampire's fangs jiggle when he talks – and eating what was supposed to be a snack but kind of grew into something larger.

I glance over at the ghost detector and see a large dot representing a spirit supposedly sitting next to me. The one-word comment is "dinner." "Nope," I say aloud. "It's too late for dinner."

The word suddenly changes to "meal." I look at the spread of food before me and must admit it's more a meal than a snack. "OK, you got me there," I say.

I'm messing with a computer app my brown-eyed girl doesn't approve of. It's a radar screen that purportedly registers the presence of dead people floating around and what they're trying to tell you. Every now and then a colored dot or two will appear on the screen and a word will pop up to convey the dead people's feelings about what's taking place around them. Of course it's meant purely for entertainment, but I'm amazed by how eerily accurate some of the comments are.

For instance, I mentioned to my wife how I'd

never show the app to my older brother. He literally drips cynicism about everything, so unless I want to endure his derisive laughter and a heaping helping of razor-sharp sarcasm I'll keep the radar to myself. Mentioning my brother by name, I asked, "Can you imagine if we told him about this?" And – seriously, no kidding – his name immediately appeared on the radar screen.

After that shocker, my wife said, "Turn that thing off. I want nothing to do with it."

She's not comfortable with either the supernatural or the paranormal. She believes ghosts have their place, and it isn't cuddling up to us as we watch *Here Comes Honey Boo Boo*. That's an inscrutable cable program about a hillbilly child who enters children's beauty pageants, which I will state categorically should be viewed only by people who carry their brains in their derrieres and bet on late-night cockfights.

I have seen my share of stupid reality shows, but this one makes anything else look Shakespearean by comparison. I have threatened to pull out my own tongue and hang myself with it if I have to watch that precocious little snot and her inbred family one more time. "As long as you don't block the TV," my wife will say.

She doesn't understand why I am more interested in the spirit world than a bunch of rednecks who say "I seen" and "I done" even more often than my neighbor Spud, who chose in high school to major in chaw and drinking beer in locked restroom stalls rather than English. She thinks flirting with the supernatural is evil and can lead to screaming, eye-clawing and involuntary pants wetting, which, if you've ever been constantly aggravated by teenagers, is nothing new.

Two more ghostly blobs appear on the radar, one so close

it's presumably sitting in my lap. I push my food further up the table and ask these dead people to kindly give me breathing space. I don't want their fetid breath on my chili cheese fries, and they're crazy if they think I'll share the barbecue pork rinds.

A word pops up on the screen: butthead. "Yeah, same to you," I retort.

"Who are you talking to?" my wife asks.

"The ghosts want my food. Tell them to get a job and buy their own."

"Do you really want to upset them?" she says. "Think of what they could do to you while you sleep tonight."

Darn it. I was really in the mood for cheese fries.

My First Sweetheart

OUR YOUNGEST WANTED TO KNOW IF HE'S ALlowed to have a girlfriend. When he asked I watched a plethora of emotions cross my wife's face in a span of two seconds. Here they are in order: nononononoNoNoNoNoNoNONONONONONO!

This is a sensitive issue for her. He's the youngest, the one who ran around in a Batman costume and a Darth Vader helmet, and the one who was caught gnawing on a stick of wood like a beaver when he was four, prompting an anxious call to the local emergency room. He was the one I taught to do a somersault, and later how to tie a necktie. And he was the tiny Cub Scout who proudly carried home a trophy for "Best Design" from the Pinewood Derby.

And now he's looking at girls, which is perfectly normal for a boy his age but unsettling to his mother, who still envisions him cuddling his binky and drinking from a juice box.

"You should wait until you're a little older," she advised him.

"But he had a girlfriend when he was twelve," the boy protested, pointing at me.

You know that disapproving glare you get from a spouse

when you've gotten carried away and talked a little too freely about your past to your kids, and then it comes back to bite you? Enough said.

Her name was Carol. She was pretty and smart and fun, and the fact that she was six inches taller than me and outweighed me by at least 15 pounds didn't discourage my infatuation. We were in sixth grade, and my developing hormones had been nagging me for some time. I let anyone who could relay the message know that she was the girl for me.

We would talk by phone or on the playground after school, and when I had the nerve I'd let her hold my sweaty hand. On Valentine's Day she gave me an Elton John 45 record I liked and I gave her a cheap box of candy hearts, an embarrassing gift but one I had scraped to buy. At a school-sponsored skating party I grew jealous and pouty over the time she spent talking to other male classmates, so she grabbed my hand and we did a lap around the rink to validate our togetherness. It didn't matter that I was impossible on roller skates and she had to keep me hoisted. She was my girlfriend, and my heart fluttered when she was around.

She was also my first heartache, and for about a month I moped around over losing her. She wanted a more proactive romance, one in which the boy was bolder and not afraid to kiss her, and could afford to treat her to a burger and fries. I was poor and naive and four-foot-nothing, and obviously couldn't deliver.

The day our youngest requested a girlfriend I tried to explain teenage girls to him. I said how they are incredibly fickle. For instance, how they can like a different boy every half hour, and how they can be sweet and demure, then loud and annoying. I told him how a teenage girl's mood can change from happy to downright scary in a New York minute, and told him he'd probably have to get three jobs just to support a girlfriend's lip gloss habit. I told him relationships can be complex, and have to be worked at, and even then there's no guarantee she wouldn't throw him over in a week for someone else.

"Yeesh," he said, looking uncertain. "Are adult women that fickle, too?"

I looked directly into my wife's eyes and told him, "Absolutely not."

I know what side my bread is buttered on.

Germs and Snickers Bars

SO ANYWAY, THE ARTICLE I'M READING LISTS some of the germiest places on Earth, and I'm mortified over one that surprised me.

I knew all the usual suspects – toilet seats, door handles, kitchen sinks and sponges. But then I saw the one I didn't expect, the one that affects me on a daily basis: my wife's purse. According to the article, stick your hand in a used purse and you may as well swallow the Ebola virus whole, and while you're at it snort a staph infection.

Now, I'm not saying I dip into my brown-eyed girl's purse every other minute. I consider it her private sanctum, where she can keep things from me like spare pens she knows I'll misplace or the ATM card, which she trusts me with about as far as she can throw my cousin Junie, who lives on peanut butter fudge. Because of that I'm forced to dig my hand into my beloved's purse and go fishing for spare change at the bottom to buy a newspaper or the junk food I sneak behind her back.

That's a dicey endeavor at best, because her purse is jam-packed with stuff probably dating back to the Paleozoic Era. She never throws anything away, so I know practically for sure that if a forensic team donned HAZMAT gear and climbed inside her purse they would find Amelia Earhart, everything ever sucked into the Bermuda Triangle and a community of pygmies.

Now and then she'll say it's time to clean her purse out, so the boys and I have to move all the furniture into another room to give her the necessary space. Then she'll upend the purse and we'll all run for cover, because the last time she cleaned it a herd of buffalo reported missing in Montana came trampling out and stomped our feet. But usually what falls out is an endless cascade of personal and household detritus that fills every available nook and cranny and eventually pushes through the ceiling. One time it took our boys three hours to climb the pile of junk and plant an American flag on top. We laughed and compared it to Mt. Everest, but my wife didn't think that joke was even a little funny.

Now I'm finding out that every time I've ever groped my way though the hundreds of layers in that purse germs have swarmed my hand and likely dashed up my arm into my armpit, where they could latch onto lymph glands and take an express ride through my body.

And heaven knows what kind of germs are percolating in that handbag, what with her tendency to absentmindedly shove all manner of things in there. That includes half-eaten sandwiches or fast food items from lunch, which she'll discover two months later mixed in among dozens of half-used lipsticks and yellowed receipts. By that time, and without refrigeration, the food has mutated into indescribably terrifying, hairy things that can actually walk and make gurgling noises.

After reading about germy purses I am suddenly noticing

what could be a scurvy rash on my purse-dipping hand, and in fact it has started to itch. I show my wife the germy purse article and my possibly scurvy hand, and give her my best accusatory look, the one I use when I break something and try to blame it on someone else.

She tells me I don't have a rash, and besides, if anyone had a rash from germy purse dipping it would be her. Then she tells me if I don't want to worry about purse germs I should stop rooting around in hers all the time for spare change, which she knows I use to buy junk food because I'm such a lousy sneaker-arounder. I counter by bragging that I'm in fact a great sneaker-arounder because I have had twenty-seven Snickers bars hidden in my underpants drawer for a week and she didn't know. To which she smiles wickedly, causing me to run panicked to the hiding place.

Twenty-six of them are missing. I hope they give her a rash.

Is it the Electric Bill or the Federal Deficit?

OPENED OUR ELECTRIC BILL THE OTHER DAY, and next thing I knew my wife was reviving me.

"Wake up!" she shouted, slapping my face harder than I thought was necessary. "We can't afford for you to faint and miss work!" Then she dumped a bucket of cold water on me, which I secretly suspect she knew wasn't necessary since I was already up and reaching for aspirin.

"How'd it get that high?" I demanded, pushing back my wet hair and waving the dripping bill. "Who the heck used all this electricity?"

She looked at me the way a person does who is facing a lion and wishing they had a high-powered tranquilizer gun. But I wanted to know where all the juice is going. It could be that power-sucking hair dryer of hers. It sounds like a Level Five hurricane, and I know for a fact it can blow away a medium-sized cat who was warned to stay out of the toilet water.

Or it might be her laptop computer, which always needs re-charging because she spends so much time playing games on it rather than digging studiously into her online classes. She tries to pretend she's hard at schoolwork when she's actually playing three-dimensional mahjong on a game site. That becomes mostly obvious when she claims to be memorizing parts of the human endocrine system but suddenly pumps her fist and yells, "Y-E-S-S-S! A new high score!"

I don't want to cast aspersions, especially because I don't actually know what an aspersion is, but I think the real culprit is the 24/7 zombie Splatterathon that goes on between the boys. At any given time they have game system consoles in their hands, and the sounds of really liquidy, gross splats reverberate through the house from their television screens. And it never ends, because the zombie-splattering games they're playing apparently restock from Bucket O' Zombies Inc. or some other wholesale warehouse specializing in the undead.

What all of this means is that my brown-eyed girl has become "The Enforcer." From here on she will scrutinize all electrical use and put down her size eight foot when she thinks someone is overusing. She's already cut back the heat, and rigged the thermostat with explosives in case someone (me) gets the crafty idea to turn it back up.

"But I'm cold," I whine pitifully, and show her the goosebumps on my arms. "And I'm almost positive you're not allowed to freeze me like this. There's a law about this somewhere, and I'm going to the toasty library to look it up."

She's wrapped in her comfy robe and sipping a steaming cup of peppermint tea. "Try getting out of those short sleeves and gym shorts and bundle up, Einstein. This isn't the Sahara, it's winter in the Midwest."

I don't care, I tell her. I'm the head of this household, and that gives me certain inalienable rights. I always get the last ice cream bar in the box, regardless of whether it's that tasteless, no-fat, fake chocolate kind she buys that, instead of, I'd rather eat a handful of dead houseflies. I always get control of the television remote after 8 p.m., even if the boys are in the middle of watching the 56th repeat one of their insipid shows that could drive a dad to bang his head with ball peen hammers. And I'm always allowed to be warm, even if the house is hot enough to melt the pets' jingle toys.

"Hey, you're the one who cried over the electric bill," my wife said defensively.

"Yeah, but I cry over everything," I protested. "Who told you to take me seriously?"

She held up the bill. "No, you were right. This puppy needs to be lowered or we'll end up living in the forest like Robin Hood. Do you want to live in the forest like Robin Hood?"

Only if I don't have to wear the tights and funny hat. The sword would be fun, though.

Mow the Lawn or Eat off Your Hands

LAWN MOWER SEASON HAS BLOSSOMED AT MY house, and the boys' usual attempts to avoid it fill the spring air.

With the advent of warming weather our lawn is becoming shaggy. I noticed that the other day when I stepped on the grass and couldn't see my feet. So I announce it's time to oil up the mower and fill it with gas. You'd think I was asking the boys to chew off their own hands.

"I think the mower's busted," the youngest says.

This is his typical preemptive strike. "I think it's fine," I say.

"No, I definitely think it's busted," he argues. "Let me take a look."

"So you can sabotage it?" I ask. "I'm surprised, this early in the season. You usually wait a couple more weeks."

Guilt crosses his face. "Are we at least going to get something for doing this?"

"Yes," I answer. "You can continue living in my house and eating my food."

I've put in my time with the mower, countless Friday

evenings and Saturday mornings plowing through an endless lawn with a cheap model that occasionally clogs. In the words of John Kennedy, it's time to pass the torch – or in this case, the gas can – to a new generation.

When they were younger they actually wanted to mow the lawn. I would lower the hand grip to near their level and let them take turns standing directly in front of me and helping me push. This would make them feel grown up and important, and that feeling would last for one, maybe two passes before they realized it was actually work and ran off to play in the shade.

When they grew older and became stronger than me, I decided it was time to relinquish the chore.

"How come we have to do it?" they bellowed.

"You mean beside the fact that it teaches you responsibility and a work ethic?" I asked. "Then how about because I'm the dad and I'm allowed to make you?"

It's no different than when I was a kid. Come Saturday my dad would point to our old push mower, and I'd whine, "How come I have to do it?" and he'd reply, "Because cutting the grass beats the punishment you'll get if you don't," and I had to admit he had a point.

My dad believed chores taught you discipline and helped develop character, and if you didn't agree with that, why, he would find ways to change your mind, like a lethal warning glare that advised you to knock off the sulky attitude and get to work.

I'd delay as long as I could with an extra glass of Tang for energy, three trips to the bathroom and what I pretended were casual, uninterested peeks at the television, but eventually my stalling wore thin.

So I'd angrily push around the old mower, a manual model that preceded gas mowers and meant having to flex a lot more muscle and put your back into it. Well, if I had wanted to flex and strain my back and get sweaty I'd have joined a logging crew. So I would push and grumble, push and grumble, blaming my dad because I was missing a lethargic morning on the couch with my favorite Saturday cartoons and a box of Cap'n Crunch. When I got further away from the house I'd whisper a curse word and dare anybody nearby to tell on me, which made me feel wicked and dangerous even though nobody heard me over the clank of the mower blades.

You can't hear grumbling over the noise of our mower, either, but you can see the boys' mouths moving in a continuous diatribe against me and what they consider my heartlessness. If you focus, sometimes you can actually read their lips: "Missing all my shows because the stupid lawn needs mowing." (Expletive)! "And I dare anybody to tell him I said that! Next thing you know, he'll want me to hang from the roof by my fingers to clear the gutters!"

Yes, I will. But his mother will ruin it by letting him use a ladder.

Jalapenos Make My Skin Smoke

So anyway, I keep munching my salad and politely nodding my head, but I'm wondering when exactly this went wrong.

"He was a big guy, big and brawny," she says enthusiastically. "What shoulders. And he had these dreamy blue eyes that gave me the shivers. Look, I'm getting goose bumps just talking about them."

"Uh-huh," I say, and spear a tomato wedge onto my fork.

"He had this restored '65 Mustang convertible, candy-apple red," she continues. "He'd fire it up to eighty and we'd just fly, laughing and listening to a CD mix he burned just for me."

"No kidding," I comment, wishing I had something stronger to drink.

"For Christmas that year, he gave me a floor-length leather jacket, and diamond earrings that were actually too big to wear," she says, sighing at the memory. "He knew how to treat a girl."

"What a guy," I agree. I'm twenty-something single, and not exactly lighting fires anywhere, so I agree to this lunch. It's a blind date, my first ever. I take an extra-long shower with manly-smelling soap, and even exfoliate, until it starts hurting and making me whimper. I put on a pair of khakis and a shirt with no armpit stains, and chew an entire pack of this excessively minty gum which completely clears my sinuses and makes my nose whistle. I run the Gremlin through a car wash, and spend twenty minutes scraping the accumulation of bugs from the windshield. As final touches, I slick my hair and brush my tongue.

Man, am I hot.

We meet at the designated restaurant. She has cascading hair, intense brown eyes and jeans tight enough to maim. While we're shown to our table I slink my hand behind me to double-check that I haven't forgotten my wallet.

Be cool, I tell myself. She didn't look at you and run, which is always a good sign. Just be cool, and don't come on too strong. Not like that last date, when you tried to pass yourself off as Erik Estrada's cousin.

I discreetly wipe my sweaty palms on my shirt and wonder how to initiate a conversation. Turns out, it's not necessary.

"I like this place," she says, admiring the room. "Me and my ex ate here a lot."

"Oh," I reply.

"He loved the steakburger. You oughta try it. He had 'em put jalapenos all over it."

Jalapenos make my skin smoke.

"He was a nice enough guy, but he had a little problem with forgery," she says.

"Really," I comment as red flags start appearing and flapping in my face.

The waitress brings our salads. My blind date has ordered the super-deluxe house special that costs a week's salary.

"Now, my other ex liked Italian food," she says, poking at a mushroom. "That guy was crazy for me. We moved in together a week after we met. He brought home this kickin' stereo system with five-foot speakers. When the cops showed up to arrest him for stealing it, I told them, 'Keep your hands off my man!' and smashed one of them with a beer bottle. The good news is, my probation ends next month."

"Wow," I say, thinking a kidney punch would be just as much fun.

Her third ex was the guy with the Mustang. She is just getting to the part about the huge diamond earrings when the waitress comes back with our food, prime rib and lobster for her and a ham and cheese with french fries for me.

"You seem okay," my blind date says fetchingly. "I like a guy who brushes his tongue. You living with anybody right now?"

"Can I get you anything else?," the waitress asks just then.

"Yes, please," I say. "Where is the restroom?"

The window is too small, so I'm going out through the ceiling tile. I'll bet none of her exes ever did that.

The Tatooed Lady at Age 75

NOT THAT IT'S MY BUSINESS, BUT I'VE BEEN SEEing more and more young people with tattoos, and I'm wondering about their futures. No, I don't have any tattoos, and good luck trying to talk me into it. I once watched a young woman get a four-leaf clover inked just above her bellybutton, and all I remember was a vicious little needle constantly jabbing her, and her repeated exclamation: "Ow! Ow-w-w! %*&#@, OW!"

And she was no lightweight, because on top of the eight other tattoos I could actually see she also had about three million exposed piercings, and at least half of those piercings had their own piercings. With all those holes all she probably has to do to water plants is stand near them and drink a glass of water.

When I was a kid the only people who had tattoos were sailors, Army guys and the kind of women my mother warned me about touching or even breathing their air. This man in my neighborhood everybody called Knock-Knock (ask him, "Who's there?" and, boy howdy, you'd find out) had a tattoo on his arm of a lady wearing the kind of skimpy underwear I got smacked for looking at in clothing catalogs.

When he flexed his muscles she would do the mambo, and all of my Catholic sensibilities would fly right out the window. After one of these hootchie-cootchie shows I ran home and drew the same lady on my arm with a permanent marker and made her mambo for my parents. After about 40 whacks on my backside and an extended stay in my bedroom I guessed maybe I shouldn't have.

Years later, when I was an over-eager bachelor on the prowl who couldn't even score a date with one of those toothless, wrinkled Eskimo women in National Geographic, a co-worker showed me a photo of her tattoo. It was a sexy, curvy snake running from her thigh to her ankle, with one of the Keebler elves in its jaws. "Hold the phone," I shouted, "What else have you got slithering around your body?" Later, during my mandated sensitivity training session, I learned that wasn't appropriate.

I've seen the colorful "tramp stamps" on women's lower backs and the dragons on men's calves, and I saw this big bruiser with a head the size of Barbie's Dream House who had a UPC code etched onto the back of his neck. It was fascinating, and I asked if he was on sale that week, and he actually laughed before throwing me down a flight of stairs.

What I'm curious about is, what's the deal going to be when they outgrow their rebelliousness and look to get a career position? I mean, it's probably tough for a prospective employer to take someone seriously who shows up at a job interview tattooed with eight balls on his hands and bright orange and yellow flames down his arms.

And what about when their bodies change or get older? I knew a pregnant woman with an eyeball tattoo on her stomach, and by the time she delivered the baby it had grown to the size of a hubcap and gave the entire hospital staff nightmares for a year.

You have to wonder how, say, a butterfly will look when the person is 75 years old and has a good case of the crags and creases. For that matter, how any of these tattoos will look when they become all wrinkled and pruny. I would hate to be that age and have to explain that what looks like a troll plastered on my neck was a tattoo of Halle Berry before it shriveled up.

Although you have to admit, it's going to be very interesting in coming years, when a bunch of white-haired, creaking senior citizens will be walking around with tattooed barbed wire and trailing vines all over their bodies, and skulls and lightning bolts showing through their sheer support hose. If my parents had looked like that when I grew up I can guarantee I'd be heavily medicated and in intense therapy today.

I wonder just when the young will wake up to the full implications of this ongoing fashion trend. I would pay big money to watch as the realization finally slams them between the eyes.

Note to Self - Socks First, Shoes Second

"WHAT THE $%&#! WERE YOU THINKING?" my dad used to ask after I pulled some boneheaded stunt that left his jaw unhinged and scraping the floor. "Do you have a lick of common sense in what passes for your brain?"

My mother wasn't as direct with her disappointment, but would shake her head and say, "Oh David" in a drawn-out way that would make me feel two inches tall. Then she'd defer back to my dad, but by then he was so angry his lecture would come out as incomplete sputters: "Never seen anything like ... Can't understand why you would ... Didn't raise you to ... Can only imagine what the neighbors ... Oughta knock you from here to ..."

This happened often enough that people thought he stuttered around me. The truth was, he was counting down the days until I decided to live on my own. Every morning he'd X off another day on the kitchen calendar, and mumble, "Maybe today. Please let it be today." When I finally moved out he sent a press release to the city newspaper and radio and television stations with HALLELUJAH!! printed five inches high at the top.

See, I wasn't exactly a problem child, but I could drive him eight kinds of crazy. I wasn't loafing unemployed around the house, knocking back rotgut, smoking unfiltered cigarettes and stealing his credit card to order do-it-yourself body piercing kits off home shopping networks. (That was my sister.) I was basically a good kid with reasonable manners who regularly brushed his teeth and kept the acne under control. But my complete lack of anything resembling common sense was apparently enough reason to shoot his blood pressure to record-high levels making his eyes glow red in the dark. It was a sight that – even though none of us will admit to it until we've had a few drinks – has lead us children to keep on night lights as adults.

Now the frustration is on the other dad, so to speak, as the boys continue their development in the Exasperating Teenager Department. Believe me, their own egregious lack of common sense can make my neck veins throb and dance the Electric Slide.

"I can't open the door!"

The 15-year-old stands on the front porch cradling a bag from the grocery store we asked him to fetch from the car. He is shouting through a window. "Shift the bag to one hand and use the other to open the door," I call out patiently.

He follows my instructions, then shouts, "I still can't open the door!"

"Why not?"

"Because I'm right-handed, and I'm holding the bag with that hand!"

I look at his mother with my pained "Is He Serious" expression, but she just shrugs.

"Then shift the bag to your left hand," I say.

"Oh – hey! That'll work," he says with wonder.

He enters the house, and gusty weather blows the screen door against the porch railing.

"Quick, close that before the cats get out," I say.

"I can't."

"Why?" I ask wearily.

"Duh. Because I'm holding a bag of groceries in both hands again," he answers with his patented teen sarcasm.

"For the love of –" I begin, then stop to do calming breathing exercises. "Shift the bag to one hand – your left hand – then use the other hand, your right hand, to close the door."

He assesses my instructions. "Oh – hey! That'll work."

Meanwhile, the middle child stomps into the room. "I want to cook something."

"Be my guest," I say.

"Where do I find pans?"

"Where do you think you'll find them?"

"I don't know," he snaps. "I'm not a chef."

I sigh. "How about the kitchen?"

Realization dawns on his face. "Yeah, okay."

"Calm down," my wife tells me. "You don't exactly corner the market on common sense yourself. And for the record, you're supposed to put your socks on first, then your shoes."

Oh, hey – that'll work.

Lou-why Lou-why, OH NO, Baby, me gotta go!

SO ANYWAY, I'M AT THIS PARTY, HANGING AROUND the keg, wearing my tight velour shirt printed with monkeys that I think shows off my pectorals, but with my skinny twenty-something frame only makes me look like Skeletor with bad taste.

It's later in the evening, when things are mellow and winding down, but I'm still hopeful one of the many girls here ignoring me will say, "Nice pectorals," and then we'll dirty dance and fall in love.

Ronny is acting as deejay, and he's been spinning the latest '80s stuff, and I've been getting down with my bad self, but so far no luck. Ronny's been hanging around the keg, too, so he'll play half a song, then change his mind. You'll be listening to Bon Jovi living on a prayer, and suddenly there's a long RRRRRR! as the needle is pulled across, permanently scratching the record, and then suddenly Boy George is singing instead, asking do you really want to hurt him and make him cry. And honestly, yes, you do.

So I figure that's the end of the good music, and start to put on my coat, which a bunch of guys were using as a hockey puck during an impromptu game in the kitchen, when I stop cold.

Ronny, who everybody knows has the attention span of a ferret, has changed the record again (RRRRRR!) only this time he's hit the mother lode. Somehow he's managed to find a copy of *Louie Louie*, one of the greatest songs in the world.

"Oh – my – GAWD!" I scream, because although two adult beverages should be my limit I'm 21 and stupid, so there you are. The opening chords alone (Duh duh duh – duh duh-duh duh duh – duh duh) make the hair on my arm stand at attention. It's *Louie Louie*, the ultimate party song, and the epitome of everything I stand for as a guy with velour monkeys all over his shirt. And I know all the words.

"I know all the words!" I yell to no one in particular, and that seems like a really big deal to me, because no one knows all the words to *Louie Louie*. It was sung by the Kingsmen, an early '60s group that sounded as though it had also hung around a keg all night, so that when they sing all you can understand is the chorus, "Louie, Louie," followed by a bunch of mumbo-jumbo. But that doesn't matter; so long as you know the *Louie Louie* part you can kind of sing along.

"I know all the words!" I repeat in case no one heard me yell it at the top of my lungs the first time. "Who wants to hear all the words?"

Apparently, no one, because everyone goes about their business eating cheesy dip and gyrating on the makeshift dance floor near the sofa and playing a raucous game of cards.

Now my feelings are hurt, because I do a really awesome *Louie Louie*, just like the Kingsmen, who (no kidding) recorded it in their studio restroom because the acoustics over the commode were so good. So to get everybody's attention I pull the phonograph needle from the record (RRRRRR!)

and repeat, at an ear-splitting decibel, "Who wants to hear all the words to *Louie Louie*?"

Scott is giving me a ticked-off look that means he only invited me to the party because we're cousins, and if I don't settle down he'll tie me to the couch. But now I have attracted some interest from his guests, who have been laughing over my monkey shirt all night and pelting me with poker chips when I'm not looking.

Somewhere in the crowd someone begins a low, grumbling chant: "Lou-ie, Lou-ie," followed by Scott begging them not to encourage me. But it's too late, their attention has shifted to me, and now the chant is getting louder and more insistent: " LOU-IE! LOU-IE!"

Well, who can resist that, so I jump onto the coffee table over Scott's protests and cue Ronny to reset the record, and there it is – Duh duh duh – duh duh- duh duh duh- duh duh!

And in a screechy pitch only dogs should be able to hear, I bellow, "Lou-why, Lou-why, OH NO, baby, me gotta go! Ya ya, ya ya ya ya ya!"

This is my moment in the spotlight, velour monkeys be damned. I open my mouth to sing the first verse- "Me fine little girl, she waits for me" – but the record skips from the long scratch I gave it, so instead I keep repeating, "OH NO! Baby, me gotta go!"

"Yes, you do," someone yells, and now six muscular arms – two of them belonging to Scott – are lifting me off the coffee table and hustling me past Ronny to the front door.

Now it's years later, and I'm more mature, and tend to behave in public. But for old time's sake I'm still willing to belt out a little *Louie Louie* if anyone asks, which they never do because it hurts their dogs' ears.

David's Fourth Commandment

SO ANYWAY, SHE SETS THIS SALAD IN FRONT OF me, which she knows better than to do. It's alarmingly leafy, and not part of the comforting dinner I envisioned would save this rotten day, which nose-dived almost before I got out of bed.

I look at the greens on the plate, most of which I can't identify. They're adorned with tomato wedges and onion and carrot twirlies and grated cheese stringies, and six or seven of those oversized Italian-style croutons you could use as door stops. There's even a modicum of those fake bacon bits I'm convinced are made of spackle, even though the jar doesn't exactly mention that ingredient.

She's called the boys to the table, averting her eyes because she knows she's broken David's Fourth Commandment: *Thou shalt never, ever serve me salad.* It's in the top five of 392 commandments I presented to her along with the ring when we got engaged. It comes right after *Remember my chocolate cravings and keep them sacred,* so it's pretty important.

I watch to see if maybe this is accidental, or some kind of twisted joke, but no, she places identical salads at the other place settings. The boys come running, salivating like Pavlov's dogs, but the salad before me makes them screech to a halt so abruptly their shoes are left behind. They gasp simultaneously.

"What is this, some kind of twisted joke?" the oldest demands. "Who gave him a salad?"

"I did," my wife says.

The youngest covers his horror-stricken face. "You broke it," he says through his hands. "You broke his fourth commandment."

Okay, so it's not as if she put strychnine in my Wheaties or dropped a 10-ton weight on my head. I could actually handle those much better than this plate of plant life. She may as well have stripped foliage off the tree in our yard and garnished it with cow chips.

"I'm not eating this," I say defiantly.

"Oh, but you are," she replies.

She's wearing her familiar look of resolve, the one that says I may wear the pants in the family but she wears the crown. I hate that look, because it usually means we're going to argue, which means I'm going to dig in and sternly say things like, "I'm putting my foot down on this!" and "This discussion is over!" and yet I'm still going to lose. And I never quite know how the losing part happens, because I always use my angry husband sneer and jut out my chin like I have actual power, and sometimes pound my fist, but on a soft surface so I don't get a bruise.

"This is salad," I point out. "This is in direct violation of my fourth commandment."

"Your diet is atrocious, and I'm worried about your health," she says. "You are going to eat that salad."

She knows I don't like eating leaves. Just like she knows I don't like wearing a tie or figuring out the family finances or people touching me with their grimy feet. But she also knows that mentioning concern for my well-being is a shrewd way to suck the wind out of my protests.

"So, you want to play dirty?" I counter. "Bring it on."

Apparently, she plans to. She sets a bottle of salad dressing in front of me, and audaciously uses my own line against me – "This discussion is over!" – and gives me her wicked That Settles That smile. It's a smile you don't want to cross, because when she gets really angry she can melt polar ice caps faster than global warming. The boys, still shoeless, look from me to her, then back to me, like they're watching a particularly vicious tennis match, and I know what they're thinking: Ain't no way he's not eating that salad.

It's not often they see us go head-to-head like this. The last time was over my impulsive purchase of a nauseatingly expensive 10-in-1 kitchen gadget with a built-in nachos warmer. I personally believe you can never have enough stuff like that, but she loudly disagreed. So there were two ensuing days of snarling and caterwauling over it, and of course I returned it because jutting out my chin and punching a fluffy pillow didn't work again; and besides, the nacho warmer leaked.

I fold my arms. "I'm not eating that plate of leaves. I'm not a child, and you can't make me."

She flashes her wicked smile again. "Really? You don't think so?"

The boys are watching intently, so I have to make a stand.

"No, I don't," I respond, puffing out my chest. "You're going to remove that salad, and never do this again. And that settles that."

Long story short, the cheese stringies aren't bad, but the spackle bacon bits are going to give me indigestion.

Beyonce, Bundt Cakes and Giant Beavers

I'M STANDING IN THE GROCERY CHECKOUT LINE, holding an economy-sized Teriyaki Weenie Buddy, waiting my turn. The line is for twelve items or less, and the woman in front of me has 94 packages of Pig Lips on a Stick, which she considers one item.

She also has a Pig Lips on a Stick double coupon but it's for a competitor's brand, so she's trying to coerce the pimply high-schooler running the cash register into accepting it. The high-schooler, who is clearly afraid of the woman and her "I Eat Punks For Breakfast" T-shirt, nevertheless doesn't want misuse of a Pig Lips on a Stick double coupon going on his permanent record, and calls for the manager, who is busy trying to explain to a customer in the dairy section that head cheese may resemble roadkill but can actually taste okay if you eat it without looking at it.

I'm standing there, shifting my squishy 125-ounce package (Makes any weenie a Teriyaki Treat!) from arm to arm, perusing the magazine rack next to me, when I see something on the *Universe Weekly* front cover I have to question: *SCIENTIFIC RESEARCH PROVES GOD IS A CAPRICORN!* Accompanying this is a retouched photo of God that looks suspiciously like Harrison Ford playing golf.

Well, being a fairly intelligent person (for instance, I can spell malapropism, even if I don't know what it means) I'm pretty certain this isn't a real photo of God, and I definitely don't believe He's a Capricorn.

Now I see another headline beneath: *Woman Gives Birth to Ninja Turtle – It Says 'Cowabunga, Dude!* When Slapped By Doctor! This is where I draw the line. I know for a fact newborn babies can't talk.

The Pig Lips on a Stick woman in front of me is arguing with the store manager, saying, "What's the difference which brand of Pig Lips on a Stick I got? Here's my coupon!" But she must have a new tongue stud, because it sounds like "pih liths ah a stih," and "Heahs my kewpah." Other than that, she looks like she can whip him.

That little drama will take awhile, so I pluck the headline-grabber off the rack and find it's chock full of amazing stories. On the second page alone I start reading about aliens from Jupiter willing to zap Rush Limbaugh in the butt with a death ray, and Jack's actual beanstalk discovered in the Bermuda Triangle.

Then on Page Five there's an advice column called Ask Sexy Shonda. ("Dear Sexy Shonda, My husband was born with three nostrils, and he's also a big, fat jerk. We don't get invited to many parties. What can we do? – Sitting at home." "Dear Sitting: Your husband should learn to whistle any Beyonce song through a straw in the extra nostril. Even a jerk with talent like that will start getting invites.")

Maybe I'm wrong to disbelieve. Maybe these are stories primetime news just doesn't cover. I'm pretty sure I've never heard on CNN that chihuahuas can psychically force their masters to fetch a ball for them, which, from the looks of the suspiciously retouched photo on page four, seems to be the case. And maybe other women married to jerks with three nostrils can take Sexy Shonda's advice and live a fuller life.

So now I'm really hooked on this magazine, when I hear the Pig Lips coupon woman erupt.

"Oo tay my kewpah, oo (thenthawd)!" ("You take my coupon, you [censored]!") The pimply cashier immediately leaves to pursue a less dangerous career. The manager braces himself and says, "I'm sorry, Ma'am, we can't do that." Then the woman turns and directs her wrath at me.

"Thuths toopih thohrihs ahn reah, oo morah!" ("Those stupid stories aren't real, you moron!" in case you don't speak Tongue Stud.)

I respond, "Oh, yeah? How do you know God isn't a Capricorn?" but she's kind of big-boned so I hold Teriyaki Weenie Buddy in front of me for protection.

I've drawn everyone's attention, so I hide behind page seven, which proclaims in a headline bigger than my house: *Giant Beaver Eats Family of Four and Bundt Cake at Campsite!* I suppose it could have happened. I once read that giant beavers love a good bundt cake.

David Will Rise Like a Fiery Phoenix

My name is David. The last time I was popular was in 1992. That was the last year my name was listed among the top ten most popular names for baby boys. This is according to the Social Security Administration, which I keep calling to remind them to stock up because I'll be needing a lot of their money. Nobody gets rich in the newspaper business, unless of course you're a publisher. In that case you can afford the ritzy brand of chocolate truffle ice cream I can only stare at longingly in the supermarket freezer while I buy the cheap, ten-gallon bucket of bubble gum sherbet that tastes like Styrofoam.

Anyway, the SSA keeps track each year of the names listed on Social Security card applications for newborns. Based on 4.2 million of a recent batch, the most popular names were Jacob for boys and Emily for girls. Other top ten names included Olivia, Joshua, Abigail, Anthony, and Samantha.

I don't mind telling you I'm feeling miffed. My name was No. 13, right after Alexander and just before Ryan. Sure, that's still a relatively high place on a list that encompasses children across the United States, but the year I was born David was listed at No. 2.

And yes, I know I'm going to hear from readers with more

obscure names like Guinevere and Moonglow and Fenster and (heaven forbid) Terrazzo, and the rest of that crowd, who will call me a big baby for complaining, since they'll never rise above the alternate list.

"What does a 'David' have to gripe about?" the indignant letter to the editor will begin. "All of my life I've wanted to be a David or Joe or Mike. Be thankful for what you've got, pal, because some of us will never know the rapture associated with being even No. 13 on the list. Some of us have had to fight and claw our way up the name ladder to reach the 6,002nd position. So go cry to someone else, because we don't want to hear it. Sincerely, Goosey-Boy."

Well, excuse me my pain, Goosey, but until now David has always been stalwart on the favorite names list. A David didn't have to worry about being replaced by a Chester or an Earl, and especially not by a Binky. His name was secure among John and Joseph and Matthew and other biblical names, most of which have remained popular. Except for Cornelius, which is usually reserved for boys with flappy ears who take violin lessons.

You could always count on David to be a fixture among the popular names, the same way you can count on spoiled, bratty Hollywood starlets to stay out too late, drink too much, and end up pictured in the tabloids without their underpants or any common sense.

And remember that David means beloved, although I haven't felt that way lately. At least not since last night, when I was informed in a rather testy tone that marriage is so much more fulfilling for women when certain people stop practicing the disgusting Cro-Magnon habits they developed as a longtime bachelor, especially those that make her gag.

Paraphrasing dialogue from a favorite old movie, David is a good name, with no stuck-up about it. So why it keeps sliding down the list is confusing. Naturally, a lot of people who wouldn't admit to knowing me for even a hundred bucks (although at five hundred bucks they perk up a little) will say I'm the leading cause of my name's slow demise. That seems a bit harsh, since my reputation precedes me only locally, where I've grown accustomed to being stopped at the city limits by other Davids brandishing automatic weapons and telling me to go away.

I'd like to see David brought back to its former glory. Those were the days, when all I had to say was, "That's right, my name is David" in order to get the same level of respect as Tom Cruise before he crashed and burned. When you're relegated to No. 13 you get the leftovers. You introduce yourself as David, and people wistfully reminisce about how you actually meant something back then in the second, or hell, even tenth position. They wish you luck but walk away shaking their heads, because they know that cocky Ethan in the fourth position has been calling you What's His Name.

Well, no more. David will rise from the ashes and reclaim its former position as a name to be reckoned with. Until then, I vow to carry David with all the pride I can muster. Well, either David or What's His Name, which is at No. 2,004.

If Looks Could Kill

QUICK, CAN YOU TELL ME WHAT I'M THINKING? Apparently, my wife can. I rose to a bright, warm day and decided that civilization wouldn't crumble if I played hooky from work. I was formulating an airtight excuse to call in (Honestly, my gall bladder just fell right out!) when she gave me Look No. 27 from her repertoire.

We've been together long enough that I can translate most of her expressions, although occasionally she'll bounce a new one off me, leaving me quivering and on my guard for weeks afterward. Look No. 27, however, is not one of those "duck and cover" types, which means I didn't have to offer her favorite red licorice and dozens of foot massages in order to be forgiven.

Look No. 27 is fairly clear-cut. It says in blunt, unvarnished language, "Don't even think about it."

My immediate reaction was to blurt out, "What? I'm not doing anything." Of course, she knew that wasn't true. Her piercing mental abilities detected my dull gears grinding out the hooky idea almost before I thought of it.

She fired the look again, just to make certain it sufficiently sizzled through my retinas, then pointed at me knowingly to drive the message home. I knew it was a bad move, but my male pride made me defiantly dial my work number.

That's when she pulled out Look No. 8. You would get chills if I described that look or its meaning. Let's just say I immediately set down the phone receiver and surrendered.

I'm not sure how she came to know me so well. In my single days I always imagined myself to be a man of such smoldering mystery that the desire to try to crack my code was irresistible to women. That little fantasy ended early in our marriage, when she tossed me what would become Look No. 1: You're Easier To Read Than A Cereal Box, So Don't Try Anything.

And, believe me, I don't. Wherever I am, whatever I'm doing, she totes her Bag of Looks with her, just in case I decide to pull a fast one. I swear, she has one for every occasion: Try to watch the uncensored Victoria's Secret fashion show on cable instead of cleaning out the garage – Look No. 32; try to sneak the last of the cheesy popcorn she's saving for the kids – Look No. 19; try to blame the cats for carelessly throwing a red sock into a load of whites – Look No. 9, 20, and 66. Combined, they can give you cramps for a week.

So what I do is decide that two can play this game, and begin developing my own set of looks. I'm new at this, so I practice in front of a mirror and, false modesty aside, have to say I've got the goods. My For Crying Out Loud, Knock It Off look is better than hers, and she has no equal to my You're Actually Going To Stand There and Try To Feed Me That Garbage look. My personal favorite is my, I Can't Believe You'd Say That To Me look, a subtle but effective expression that suggests I've been mortally offended, but all could be forgiven if I can buy something really pointless and expensive for myself.

That's the one I decide to try, because I've been eyeing this really cool, tight black leather outfit at the local men's shop, a style she says is too young for me, but which I know I can squeeze into with the help of some mechanic's grease and a little prayer.

I deliberately stand near a wastebasket she's asked me for three days to empty, and sure enough, when she sees it's still overflowing she tries to level me with Look No. 42: What, Do I Have To Draw A Map For You?

I wait a few seconds, then pour on this new wounded look of mine. If I'm careful and play it just right I may get the leather outfit and those bad-ass alligator boots in the window of that pricey specialty shop nearby.

But I foolishly underestimate her ability to read me like yesterday's newspaper. Instead of remorse and an afternoon of shopping I get her Whoa, This Time You Really Stepped In It look (No. 23) which she once used to stop a cluster of deadly asteroids.

I'd use my I'm Not Afraid look but it needs more practice. I'll be back later to finish this. I have to go buy red licorice and foot massage lotion.

David J. Coehrs is a newspaper reporter and columnist living in Napoleon,Ohio, with his wife, sons and five impudent cats.

www.ingramcontent.com/pod-product-compliance
Lightning Source LLC
Chambersburg PA
CBHW051959090426
42741CB00008B/1459

* 9 7 8 1 6 1 8 0 8 0 7 5 2 *